Child Discipline in African American Families

Child Discipline in African American Families

Culturally Responsive Policies

Carla Adkison-Johnson

LEXINGTON BOOKS

Lanham • Boulder • New York • London

Published by Lexington Books
An imprint of The Rowman & Littlefield Publishing Group, Inc.
4501 Forbes Boulevard, Suite 200, Lanham, Maryland 20706
www.rowman.com

6 Tinworth Street, London SE11 5AL, United Kingdom

British Library Cataloguing in Publication Information Available

Library of Congress Cataloging-in-Publication Data

Names: Bradley, Carla, author.
Title: Child discipline in African American families : culturally responsive policies / Carla Adkison-Johnson.
Description: Lanham : Lexington Books, [2021] | Includes bibliographical references and index.
Identifiers: LCCN 2020050845 (print) | LCCN 2020050846 (ebook) | ISBN 9781793620934 (cloth) | ISBN 9781793620941 (ebook)
Subjects: LCSH: Discipline of children—United States. | African American parents. | African American families. | Child rearing—United States. | Parenting—United States.
Classification: LCC HQ770.4 .B725 2021 (print) | LCC HQ770.4 (ebook) | DDC 306.85/08996073—dc23
LC record available at https://lccn.loc.gov/2020050845
LC ebook record available at https://lccn.loc.gov/2020050846

Contents

Acknowledgments

It has been an honor and a privilege to illuminate the voices of African American parents. I thank God for providing me the opportunity to write this book. I am grateful to my husband, Dr. Phillip D. Johnson for his patience, prayers, and support. His insight into the inner lives of African Americans from a contextual humanistic perspective was instrumental in providing the theoretical foundation for this book. I am blessed to have been raised by strong and courageous parents, my mother Ms. Herscine Adkison and my father Mr. Richard Adkison. I also have relied on the support of a fun and loving extended family (sister, grandparents, uncles, aunts, nieces, nephews, and cousins). What I know about the strengths and perseverance of African American families begins and ends with them. A special thanks is also extended to my loyal friends and church community.

Finally, this book would not have been possible without the African American mothers and fathers who gave their time and fearlessly shared their child discipline practices. Even though I modified their demographic information to protect their identity, I hope I captured what they wanted helping professionals and parents in similar situations to know about rearing African American children.

Introduction

> I tell my kids, I made your mistakes, I can tell you no and yes about this because I've done it and if I'm not sure, I'm going to tell you I'm not sure . . . So I talk to them to see what they feel . . . Even if I don't like it I still listen, because it was something they felt and I had to respect that. But that's my way of trying to find a medium . . . I still expect them to do what I tell them to do.
>
> —An African American parent

The sentiments expressed by this African American parent represent the reflective yet firm tradition of child discipline in African American families. This book focuses on the disciplinary practices of African American mothers and fathers, as well as the intentional and strategic ways in which African American parents respond to child misbehavior. Research investigations that focus on the disciplinary practices of African Americans have found that African American parents use a wide variety of disciplinary techniques, with "discussions with their children" as the primary method used to address child misbehavior (e.g., Brodosky & DeVet, 2000; Horn et al., 2004; Greene & Garner, 2012; Mitchell et al., 2009; Richman & Mandara, 2013).

Disciplinary patterns in African American homes are often hierarchal in nature, meaning that verbal discussions are typically the first response and may later escalate to more coercive strategies (e.g., the withdrawal of privileges, giving the child a warning look) in order to address repeated misconduct (Adkison et. al, 2016; Doyle et al., 2016; Hawbroski & Maton, 1998; Lansford et al., 2012; McLoyd, 2019). When and if physical discipline (with an open hand or the use of a belt) is used, it is rarely handled as a stand-alone strategy (Adkison-Johnson, 2019; McLoyd et al., 2019). Rather, it is often coupled with a discussion before and after the disciplinary episode, used as a last resort (when all other disciplinary strategies have failed), and reserved for blatantly defiant child behavior (Adkison-Bradley et al., 2014; Adkison-Johnson et al., 2016; Adkison-Johnson, 2019; Belgrave & Allison, 2019; Bradley, 1998, 2000; Denby & Alford, 1996; Doyle et al., 2015; Green & Garner, 2012; Peters, 1976, 1985). These disciplinary responses are contingent upon both the age of the child as well as the context of the disciplinary episode.

CURRENT DEBATE ON CHILD DISCIPLINE

Nonetheless, many researchers have pinpointed the use of physical discipline as a "source of pathology" in African American families, even though physical discipline is the least frequently used technique and/or least frequently endorsed strategy among African American mothers and fathers (McLoyd et al., 2019; Adkison-Bradley, 2011). The basis of this assumption is largely derived from the various studies and writings that consistently show that African American mothers use or endorse physical discipline more frequently than White American mothers (e.g., Anderson, 1936; Bartz & Levine, 1972; Deater-Deckard et al., 1996; Lorber et al., 2011; Portes et al., 1986). Although researchers have acknowledged that negative outcomes from physical discipline observed in White American children is either not found or less strongly related to negative outcomes in African American children, African American disciplinary methods continue to be characterized as change-worthy (Adkison-Johnson, 2011; Fontes, 2002, 2008).

Further complicating this issue is strong support from influential organizations calling for a ban on spanking. Most notably, in 2019, the American Psychological Association (APA), the professional organization that represents psychologists in the United States, adopted a resolution opposing the use of physical punishment by parents (APA, 2019). The resolution cites numerous empirical studies that link the use of physical discipline to aggression, antisocial behaviors, and mental health problems in children (Lee et al., 2014; Gershoff & Grogan-Kaylor, 2016; Gershoff et al., 2018). Similarly, the American Academy of Pediatrics (AAP) has also issued a policy statement supporting the need for parents to avoid physical punishment and yelling at children (Sege & Siegel, 2018).

However, social scientists have documented the inadequacies of the scientific evidence underlying the APA resolution (e.g., Larzelere et al., 2010, 2018c, d; Larzelere & Baumrind, 2010). For example, in a recent issue of the *American Psychologist*, the official journal of the APA, Larzelere et al. (2019) argue that the biggest problem with the "evidence" against physical discipline cited by anti-spanking researchers is that virtually all of the studies provided only correlational (casual) evidence, and did not show a direct causal link between physical punishment and adverse outcomes in children. For a detailed examination of the most serious shortcomings of research that support spanking bans, please see Larzelere (1986), Larzelere et al. (2013), and Larzelere et al. (2017). Additionally, Rohner and Melendez-Rhodes (2019) contend that cross-cultural and intracultural evidence has shown that adverse effects (from spanking) are not often as direct or causal as reported by anti-spanking researchers. It is important to note that in my own review of the more than 100 studies referenced in the APA resolution, virtually none were conceptualized to solely analyze the disciplinary methods of African American parents.

The legal profession is likewise examining the suitability of corporal punishment. At the 2015 American Bar Association's (ABA) Mid-year Meeting, a panel of legal and clinical experts discussed the matter of child discipline and the distinction between physical discipline (spanking) and child abuse. The principle applied by most states is that parents may use "reasonable force" to discipline their children. Previous court cases have ruled that leaving a mark or bruise on the body after spanking a child does not necessarily constitute child abuse (Adkison-Johnson et al., 2016; Davidson, 1997). The panelists recognized that because many states rely on clinicians, child welfare workers, or the courts to determine what qualifies as reasonable or excessive child discipline, racial bias can be a factor in such cases (Laird, 2015). Furthermore, recent conference presentations at national meetings of the Association of Family and Conciliation Courts (AFCC) highlighted the "Anglo-centric policies" that impact the child welfare system (Larzerlere et al., 2019), as well as the cultural bias and/or lack of cultural awareness among trial lawyers and family court judges when considering the appropriateness of physical discipline (Adkison-Johnson & Payne, 2019).

SITUATION FOR AFRICAN AMERICAN PARENTS

How we think about African American families is often how we respond to them. Researchers and practitioners have noted that White American child protective service workers in particular have expressed discomfort in broaching the topic of child discipline with African American mothers and fathers (Kris & Skivenes, 2011; Gray & Nybell, 1990; Yoos et al., 1995). In fact, many African American parents are what legal scholar Roberts (2011, 2012) describes as "under surveillance" by educational and child welfare personnel who often subscribe to the automatic assumption that parenting while Black means that children are at risk of harm (Adkison-Johnson et al., 2016). Even though the most recent National Incidence Study of Child Abuse and Neglect (Sedlack et al., 2010) indicates that population differences in maltreatment are not due to the race of the parent (Russell & Cooper, 2011), African Americans are disproportionately reported by child welfare and educational professionals for suspected child abuse. National statistics show that of the *437,283* children in foster care, *193,117* were White, *99,025* were African American, and *90,688* were Hispanic (of any race) (AFCARS Report, 2018). In fact, Roberts and Sangoi (2018) report that in cities such as New York and Chicago, Black and Hispanic families constitute virtually all families under state supervision, and all children in foster care as well.

Several investigations examining the overrepresentation of children of color in the child welfare system identified a "slippery slope" leading from African American families encountering child protective services toward the loss of child custody (Curtis & Denby, 2011; Dixon, 2008; Hill, 2006; Roberts, 2002, 2018). Consequently, when African Americans lose their constitutional right to parent their children, they face a loss more severe than just the loss of care and companionship (Guggenheim & Sankaren, 2015). This rupture contravenes the process of preparing African American children to become conscious of their own being, purpose, and responsibility toward their community in a society that is hostile toward African Americans (Johnson, 2016; Noble, 1974; Peters, 1976).

The goal of this book is to provide an in-depth, contextual understanding of African American disciplinary styles. A contextual perspective of African American child discipline has thus far received limited empirically informed critical analysis which would be needed to fully comprehend how and why African American mothers and fathers use discipline to achieve their parenting goals. A sharper focus on the patterns and context of child discipline has become a professional imperative, as clinicians, child welfare workers, and legal personnel encounter increasingly diverse families. However, the routine, no-nonsense, and strategic disciplinary methods of African American mothers and fathers often cited among African American scholars continue to be marginalized in traditional psychological explanations of appropriate parenting. As a result, helping professionals are left with limited information regarding how African American parents address the normal developmental issues associated with raising children. This continued void in the literature can lead professionals in child welfare and legal settings to minimize potential cases of physical abuse, or to overpathologize and criminalize functional and strategic parenting.

As of today, the current research on African American child discipline primarily comprises data that were extracted from larger studies on various aspects of child rearing. But in this book, African American child discipline is the point of departure. Specifically, this book reviews and synthesizes several decades of important research on African American child discipline, along with examining the basic characteristics, core values, and cultural contexts that influence African American child rearing.

A key feature of this book is highlighting the voices of African American parents in conceptualizing child discipline, and the analysis is extended to include implications for culturally responsive service delivery, law, and public policy. For more than twenty-five years, I have explored the occurrence of child discipline in African American communities, and have recently completed a human subjects–approved qualitative study involving African American mothers and fathers with school-age children in the home. This data provides important insights into how African American parents are thinking right now about child-rearing objectives and child behavior expectations in a consistently changing and regularly racially threatening society. The data gives a coherent system to clinicians, child welfare workers, and legal experts to be all the more likely characterize what is *typical*, *reasonable*, and *practical* when tending to child-rearing concerns with African American parents.

MY BACKGROUND AND INTEREST IN
AFRICAN AMERICAN CHILD DISCIPLINE

Over thirty years ago, during the completion of my master's degree to become a clinical mental health counselor, I had a full-time job as a child protective services intake worker. In one particular case, I investigated an alleged physical abuse incident in which an African American mother had come home from work and whupped her twelve-year-old daughter with a belt for being caught "half naked" in the basement with her teenaged boyfriend. After I questioned the mother and father about their household rules and behavioral expectations, and also found that there were no longstanding marks or bruises on the child, the mother was required to attend parenting classes and counseling. I asked my supervisor why the mother was penalized for what I thought was a rational response to the child's misbehavior, but I did not obtain a clear answer, and was left wondering how child protective service workers viewed African American parenting. I eventually became concerned that the disciplinary practices of African American parents (including my own parents) would be perceived as problematic by the social work and mental health professions.

I was drawn to counselor education because I wanted to directly intervene in the lives of individuals and families from a developmental perspective. I was not only interested in what was wrong; rather, I wanted to highlight how African Americans coped and transcended situations in order to accomplish their goals and aspirations. When I decided to pursue my Doctorate of Philosophy in Counseling and Development, I was led to Kent State University to study under Dr. Mary Smith Arnold, who also had an interest in the ways in which African Americans disciplined their children. She died shortly after I completed my doctorate, but her guidance instilled in me the importance of understanding the context of child discipline in my work as a Professor in Counselor Education. She directed me to the seminal works of Dr. Andrew Billingsley, Dr. Marie Ferguson Peters, Dr. Robert Staples, Drs. John and Harriett McAdoo, Dr. Alvin Poussaint, and Dr. James Comer, as well as many other African American scholars who investigated or made mention of Black child-rearing and child discipline practices. She also pointed me to the works of Dr. Nancy Boyd-Franklin, Dr. Kenneth V. Hardy, Dr. Howard Stevenson, Dr. Haki Madhubuti, Dr. Na'im Akbar, and Dr. Patricia Hill-Collins in order to provide an in-depth understanding of the many psychological and environmental influences that impact African American family life.

My first series of analyses consisted of a database of 156 African American parents who represented a variety of income and educational backgrounds. I was interested in establishing benchmark data on the kinds of discipline that African American parents use, as well as how gender differences, economic variations, and the age of the child may affect their choice to utilize a specific strategy. After fifteen years, I collected data on 189 more African American parents in order to identify how African American mothers and fathers addressed repeated misbehavior in their children. My latest examination consists of in-depth interviews with African American mothers and fathers that allowed me to get an increasingly extensive picture of the most pressing behavioral concerns that they have with their school-age children. Each of these investigations had university human subjects board approval.

I also think it is worth noting that I am an African American woman who was raised by an African American mother and father with a very strong extended family system. My parents utilized a variety of disciplinary methods (including a few whuppins) in order to change my problematic behaviors (I was the type of child who always had something to say, and asked a lot of questions). Each time I was disciplined as a child (mainly between the ages of six and ten), I knew what I had done wrong, and most of the time, I was trying to skillfully avoid the expected punishments. My parents had a lot of patience, and supported my inquisitive nature.

CONCEPTUAL FRAMEWORK

Much of the psychological discourse that pertains to African Americans has portrayed them as raising children in homes where violence is predictable, fathers are absent, mothers are angry, and both parents are reckless and use disciplinary tactics that could be construed as child abuse. When social scientists are preoccupied with the practice of African Americans spanking or "whuppin" their children, it becomes easier to deny African American parents their intentional (e.g., explained behavioral expectations to child) and structured (e.g., age and context specific, hierarchical in nature) child-rearing qualities that are associated with being a competent parent (Adkison-Bradley, 2011; Johnson, 2009).

In this book, a contextual humanistic approach will be used as a lens with which to examine child disciplinary practices in African American families. A fundamental core belief of the humanistic tradition is the importance placed upon understanding each person's perception of reality in order to fully understand his or her behavior. This necessitates considering how people see things in order to comprehend what an individual expects to do, as well as what purposes and objectives they hold (Jenkins, 2004). The humanistic approach also assumes that people have the capacity to take a dialectical or bipolar approach to meaning. In other words, people have the capacity to conceptually transcend the actualities of a given reality and envision different perspectives about the ways in which things could be (Jenkins, 1995, 2004, 2005).

Choice and will are seen to be among the central aspects of human functioning. However, Johnson (2006) offers an important corrective to the traditional ways in which humanistic theory has been conceptualized in the social sciences, contending that the situation for African Americans cannot be explained primarily in terms of basic human qualities or needs. He recommends that a contextualized humanistic perspective be utilized in order to view and appreciate African Americans as being fully human. A *contextualized humanistic perspective* is a gathering notion under which a humanistic perspective, along with the worldview and experiences of African Americans, can be utilized in order to allow for understanding the humanity of African American mothers and fathers (Johnson, 2006, 2016; Personal Communication, 2020). Having a greater sense of purpose, worth, and community are central elements of this viewpoint (Johnson, 2016).

This perspective assumes that the condition of African American parents must be understood in terms of the historical reality of racism and racial oppression that manifested most vividly in the enslavement of Africans in the United States. Of course 400 years of chattel slavery had a profound effect on the lives of African American families. The African slave trade and the institution of slavery ruptured families and tribal connections, leaving indelible scars on the African continent, as well as among those who were ripped from its shores (Arnold, 2002). One of the greatest injustices of slavery was the denial that Africans possessed the capacity to love, nurture, and raise their children. However, Jenkins (1995, 2001, 2005), Johnson (2009, 2016), and Adkison-Johnson and Johnson (2019) argue that African Americans have sustained their creative and resilient parenting capacities in spite of the continually oppressive circumstances that have historically characterized them as incompetent mothers and fathers. In other words, slavery did not define African American families, nor were their parenting goals or child discipline practices a reactive response to the external conditions forced upon them.

A contextual humanistic perspective offers an important change to the typical dehumanized view of African American mothers and fathers. This perspective helps to illustrate how African American parents use their intentional, moral, spiritual, and creative abilities in rearing their children, even as hostile forces seek to undermine them.

METHOD OF DATA COLLECTION

I have included findings in this book from the entirety of my previous research (for a detailed discussion of this work, see Adkison-Bradley, 2011; Adkison-Bradley et al., 2014; Adkison-Johnson et al., 2016; Adkison-Johnson & Johnson, 2019; Bradley, 1998, 2000, 2002) alongside the featured explorations of other scholars who have noted significant findings in their quest to address the African American child discipline question. Additionally, this book contains some results of my current investigation spotlighting how African American parents are currently thinking about child discipline objectives and child behavior expectations in a consistently changing and regularly racially threatening society. I used a qualitative descriptive exploratory design in this study.

Specifically, I conducted face-to-face semi-structured in-depth interviews with thirty-six African American parents (twenty-five mothers and eleven fathers) in order to provide clear communication regarding their parenting perspectives. According to Sandelowski (2000), qualitative descriptions "are amenable to obtaining straight and largely unadorned (i.e., minimally theorized or otherwise transformed or spun) answers to questions of special relevance to practitioners and policy makers" (p. 37). The data presented in this study was collected as part of a larger research project dedicated to understanding the psychological functioning of African American parents as they grapple with raising school-age children. This data was gathered as an initial step in identifying the disciplinary practices, concerns, and goals of African American parents with school-age children. In order to be eligible, individuals had to be at least eighteen years old and have at least one preadolescent-age child who either lives with the parent(s) or lives away from the parent(s). Both parents of the child had to identify as African American as well. Recruitment consisted of posting culturally relevant fliers in the community, as well as church bulletins and newsletters. I also made presentations to family court officials and child protective services personnel, along with being interviewed about the project on the local radio station. I wanted potential participants to know that I was an African American professor, clinician, and researcher who has over twenty-five years of clinical experience in working with African American parents, and that I was invested in the success of African American families.

I was particularly sensitive to the risk (or perceived risk) involved in African American parents disclosing their disciplinary practices. Parents were advised in the informed consent documents that the state in which they live did not prohibit them from taking steps to reasonably discipline their child. I also let them know I was keenly aware that African Americans have been heavily scrutinized by child protective service agencies due to cultural bias by social workers and mental health professionals regarding child-rearing practices. However, each parent was made aware that if they did disclose an intended act of child abuse, I would report such act to child protective services. I simply wanted to encourage parents to share their feelings, concerns, and practices about disciplining their children without feeling they were being evaluated or judged. The distinction between child discipline and child abuse will be presented in chapters 5 and 6. It is important to note that each parent (whether they participated in the study or not) voiced their appreciation in understanding their hesitancy and/or reluctance toward having an open conversation about disciplining their children.

Once consent to participate was obtained, I interviewed each parent for approximately forty-five to sixty minutes in my office on campus, or at the counseling center adjacent to my office suite. All interviews were recorded and transcribed by a professional transcription service that specialized in confidential medical dictations. Demographic information is presented for the parents who participated in the study in chapters 3 and 4. Parents were instructed to list the behaviors that concerned them the most about their children, as well as the disciplinary methods they used to correct such behaviors. During the interview, I used questions from the African American Child Discipline (AACD) Survey. I created and used the AACD survey in several of my previous investigations in order to explore child discipline in African American families (for detailed survey information, see Bradley, 2000; Adkison-Johnson et al., 2016). The survey asked parents to respond to an example of a child's transgression and to identify a second response if the child repeated the same transgression. In the present study, parents were permitted to respond freely to the questions with an understanding that there was no right or wrong answer. They were also encouraged to cite examples of their own child's behavior, or anything else that they wanted to share concerning child discipline.

The method used to analyze the interview data was Braun and Clarke's (2006) six phases of thematic analysis: (1) familiarize yourself with the data; (2) generate initial codes; (3) search for themes; (4) review themes; (5) define and name themes; and (6) produce a report. I listened to each interview in order to ensure that the information was transcribed accurately. At the time of checking the transcripts for accuracy, I removed all identifying data and made notes on the transcripts to catch non-verbal behaviors (smiling, tears, and reflective silence) (Thompson et al., 2013). I reviewed each transcript several times in order to become fully acquainted with the data, and also performed the initial coding and identification of themes.

In order to enhance validity of the findings, I used a team of African American professors and doctoral students with qualitative methods training to independently code randomly selected transcripts. Utilizing observers working independently of one another yields reliability data whose reliability can be measured (Krippendorff, 2019). The independent observers (transcript reviewers) and I independently proposed a list of themes to categorize and organize each statement (Thompson et al., 2013). Only the themes that reached a level of agreement among all reviewers were used for this book. The qualitative analysis of the interviews generated themes for African American mothers, fathers, and both parents either living with or living away from their children. Specifically, the case examples and/or current data utilized in chapters 3, 4, and 5 are a compilation of the findings from this study.

One more thing is that I have purposely limited the amount of descriptive information about the sample, as well as the specifics and location of the study. Pseudonyms have been used in order to protect the identities and the exact occupation and ages of the participants and their children have also been changed to protect the parents who graciously agreed to contribute to this study.

HOW THIS BOOK IS STRUCTURED

Chapter 1 provides a historical examination of the seminal writings and studies that are critical in properly analyzing the legacy of African American child rearing in general, and African American disciplinary practices in particular. The chapter discusses the core values that underline AACD with fundamental child-rearing responsibilities, such as racial socialization.

Chapter 2 provides a historical as well as present-day depiction of African American women as mothers, and a review of the pertinent studies focusing primarily on the disciplinary strategies used by African American mothers. The last section of the chapter highlights findings from my current investigation into how African American mothers are addressing misbehavior of school-age children.

Chapter 3 illuminates the research on African American fathers regarding their parenting activities, along with a detailed examination of their distinct disciplinary patterns and practices. A key feature of this chapter is the identification of problematic child behaviors from the viewpoint of African American men, as well as the methods that they use in order to establish culturally appropriate conduct in their children.

Chapter 4 explores child discipline from a co-parenting perspective. Specifically, this chapter examines how parents present a united front in terms of addressing behavioral problems with their children.

Chapter 5 provides an in-depth analysis and further recommendations for culturally responsive child discipline policies. A framework is provided in order to assist social workers and clinicians with culturally competent service delivery.

Chapter 6 provides a unique opportunity for readers to see how attorneys grapple with the child discipline question. Contributing author E. Dorphine Payne, JD, is a seasoned trial lawyer who presents a compelling discussion regarding how attorneys challenge the presumption that African Americans are reckless disciplinarians.

Finally, Chapter 7 summarizes the key points in the book, offers areas for future research, and delivers implications for professional training and supervision.

REFERENCES

Adkison-Bradley, C. (2011). Seeing African Americans as competent parents: Implications for marriage and family counselors. *The Family Journal, 19*, 307–313.

Adkison-Bradley, C., Terpstra, J., & Dormitorio, B. (2014). Child discipline in African American families: A study of patterns and context. *The Family Journal, 22*, 198–205.

Adkison-Johnson, C. (2019). *Exploring Child Discipline: Effectiveness of a Counseling Group for African American Parents*. Chicago, IL: American Psychological Association Annual Convention.

Adkison-Johnson, C., & Payne, D. (2019). *Criminality Vs. Intentionality: An Examination of the Disciplinary Practices of African American Parents*. Association of Family and Conciliation Courts 56th Annual Conference. Toronto, Canada.

Adkison-Johnson, C., Terpstra, J., Burgos, J., & Payne, D. (2016). African American child discipline: Differences between mothers and fathers. *Family Court Review, 54*(2), 203–220.

AFCARS. (2018). Adoption and FosterCare Analysis and Reporting System (AFCARS) FY2018data². https://www.acf.hhs.gov/cb

American Psychological Association (APA). (2019). Resolution on Physical Discipline of Children by Parents. www.apa.org/about/policy/physical-discipline.pdf

Anderson, J. E. (1936). *The Young Child in the Home.* White House Conference on child Health and Protection, Committee on the infant and Pre-school Child. Appleton-Century, New York.

Arnold, M. (2002). Counseling African American families in a post-modern era. In Lipford-Sanders & Bradley, C. (Eds.), *Counseling African American Families* (pp. 1–10). Alexandria, VA: American Counseling Association.

Bartz, K. W., & Levine, E. S. (1978). Child rearing by Black parents: A description and comparison to Anglo and Chicano parents. *Journal of Marriage and the Family, 40*, 709–719.

Belgrave, F. Z., & Allison, K. W. (2019). *African American Psychology: From Africa to America*. Thousand Oaks: Sage Publication.

Bradley, C. R. (1998). Child rearing in African American families: A study of disciplinary methods used by African American parents. *Journal of Multicultural Counseling and Development, 26*, 273–281.

Bradley, C. R. (2000). The disciplinary practices of African American fathers: A closer look. *Journal of African American Men, 5*, 43–61.

Braun, V., & Clarke, V. (2006). Using thematic analysis in psychology. *Qualitative Research in Psychology, 3*(2), 77–101.

Brodsky, A. E., & DeVet, K. A. (2000). You have to be real strong: Parenting goals and strategies of resilient, urban, African American, single mothers. *Journal of Prevention and Intervention in the Community, 20*, 157–178.

Curtis, C., & Denby, R. (2011). African American children in the child welfare system: Requiem or reform. *Journal of Public Child Welfare, 5*(1), 111–137.

Davey, M., Niño, A., Kissil, K., & Ingram, M. (2012). African American parents' experiences navigating breast cancer while caring for their children. *Qualitative Health Research, 22*(9), 1260–1270.

Davison, H. (1997). The legal aspects of corporal punishment in the home: When does physical discipline cross the line to become child abuse. *Children's Legal Rights Journal, 18*, 20–29.

Day, R. D., Peterson, G. W., & McCraken, C. (1998). Predicting spanking on younger and older children by mothers and fathers. *Journal of Marriage and the Family, 60*, 79–94.

Deater-Deckard, K., Dodge, K., Bates, J., & Pettit, G. (1996). Physical discipline among African American and European American mothers: Links to children's externalizing behaviors. *Developmental Psychology, 32*(6), 1065–1072.

Denby, R. W., & Alford, K. A. (1996). Understanding African American discipline styles: Suggestions for effective social work intervention. *Journal of Multicultural Social Work, 4*(3), 81–98.

Dixon, J. (2008). The African American child welfare act: A legal redress for African American disproportionality in child protection cases. *Berkeley Journal of African American Law and Policy, 10*, 109–313.

Doyle, O., Clark, T., Cryer-Coupet, Q., Nebbitt, V., Goldston, D., Estroff, S., & Magan, I. (2015). Unheard Voices: African American Fathers Speak About Their Parenting Practices. *Psychology of Men & Masculinity, 16*(3), 274–283.

Doyle, O., Estroff, S., Goldston, D., Dzirasa, E., Fontes, M., & Burriss, A. (2014). "You gotta have a good help mate": African American fathers' co-parenting experiences. *Psychology of Men & Masculinity, 15*(4), 377–386.

Doyle, O., Magan, I., Cryer-Coupet, Q., Goldston, D., & Estroff, S. (2016). "Don't wait for it to rain to buy an umbrella": The transmission of values from African American fathers to sons. *Psychology of Men & Masculinity, 17*(4), 309.

Fontes, L. A. (2002). Child discipline and physical abuse in immigrant Latino families: Reducing violence and misunderstandings. *Journal of Counseling and Development, 80*, 31–40.

Fontes, L. A. (2008). *Child Abuse and Culture: Working with Diverse Families.* New York: Guilford Press.

Gershoff, E., & Grogan-Kaylor, A. (2016). Spanking and child outcomes: Old controversies and new meta-analyses. *Journal of Family Psychology, 30*(4), 453.

Gershoff, E., Sattler, K., & Ansari, A. (2018). Strengthening causal estimates for links between spanking and children's externalizing behavior problems. *Psychological Science, 29*(1), 110–120.

Gray, S. S., & Nybell, L. M. (1990). Issues in African American family preservation. *Child Welfare, 56*, 513–523.

Greene, K., & Garner, P. (2012). African American mothers' disciplinary responses: Associations with family background characteristics, maternal childrearing attitudes, and child manageability. *Journal of Family Economic Issues, 33*, 400–409.

Guggenheim, M., & Sankaran, V. S. (2015). *Representing Parents in Child Welfare Cases: Advice and Guidance for Family Defenders.* Chicago, IL: American Bar Association Book Publishing.

Hawbroski, F. A., Maton, K. L., & Grief, G. L. (1998). *Beating the Odds: Raising Academically Successful African American Males.* New York, NY: Oxford University Press.

Hill, R. (2004). *Black Overrepresentation: Synthesis of Research Findings.* Presentation to the Michigan Advisory Committee on the Overrepresentation of Children of Color in Child Welfare.

Hill, R. B. (2006). *Synthesis of Research on Disproportionality in Child Welfare: An Update.* Washington, DC: The Casey-CSSP Alliance for Racial Equity.

Horn, I. B., Cheng, T. L., & Joseph, J. (2004). Discipline in the African American community: The impact of socioeconomic status on beliefs and practices. *Pediatrics, 113*, 1236–1241.

Jenkins, A. H. (1995). *Psychology and African Americans: A Humanistic Approach* (2nd ed.). Needham Heights: Allyn & Bacon.

Jenkins, A. H. (2001). Individuality in cultural context: The case for psychological agency. *Theory & Psychology, 11*(3), 347–362.

Jenkins, A. H. (2005). Creativity and resilience in the African American experience. *The Humanistic Psychologist, 33*(1), 25–32.

Johnson, P. D. (2006). Counseling Black men: A contextualized humanistic approach. *Counseling and Values, 50*, 187–196. doi:10.1002/j.2161-007X.2006.tb00055.x

Johnson, P. D. (2016). Somebodiness and its meaning to African American men. *Journal of Counseling and Development, 94*, 333–344.

Krippendorff, K. (2019). Content analysis: An introduction to its methodology (4th ed.). Thousand Oaks, CA: Sage Publication.

Kriz, K., & Skivenes, M. (2011). How child welfare workers view their work with racial and ethnic minority families: the United States in contrast to England and Norway. *Children and Youth Services Review, 33*, 1866–1874.

Laird, L. (April, 2015). Experts debate line between spanking and abuse. *American Bar Association Journal, 60*, 65.

Lansford, J. E., Wager, L. B., Bates, J. E. Dodge, K. A., & Pettit, G. S. (2012). Parental reasoning, denying privileges, yelling and spanking: Ethnic differences and associations with child externalizing behavior. *Parenting: Science and practice, 12*, 42–56.

Larzelere, R. E. (1986). Moderate spanking: Model or deterrent of children's aggression in the family? *Journal of Family Violence, 1*, 27–35.

Larzelere, R. E., & Baumrind, D. (2010). Are spanking injunctions scientifically supported? *Law & Contemporary Problems, 73*, 57–88. http://scholarship.law.duke.edu/lcp/vol73/iss2/4/

Larzelere, R. E., Cox, R., & Smith, G. L. (2010). Do nonphysical punishments reduce antisocial behavior more than spanking? A comparison using the strongest previous causal evidence against spanking. *BMC Pediatrics. 10*(10). Online publication. doi:1186/1471-2431-10-10. http://www.biomedcentral.com/1471-2431/10/10

Larzelere, R. E., Cox, R. B., Jr., & Mandara, J. (2013). Responding to misbehavior in young children: How authoritative parents enhance reasoning with firm control. In R. E. Larzelere, A. S. Morris, & A. W. Harrist (Eds.), *Authoritative Parenting: Synthesizing Nurturance and Discipline for Optimal Child Development* (pp. 89–111). Washington, DC: American Psychological Association Press.

Larzelere, R. E., Fuller, J., Cox, R. B., Jr., & Saini, M. (2018a). *Is Spanking a Victim of Scholar-Advocacy Bias?* Research presented at the Association of Family and Conciliation Courts, Pittsburgh, PA.

Larzelere, R. E., Gunnoe, M. L., Ferguson, C. J., & Roberts, M. W. (2019). The insufficiency of the evidence used to categorically oppose spanking and its implications for families and psychological science: Comment on Gershoff et al. (2018). *American Psychologist, 74*(4), 497–499. http://dx.doi.org/10.1037/amp0000461

Larzelere, R. E., Knowles, S. J., Henry, C. S., & Ritchie, K. L. (2018b). Immediate and long-term effectiveness of disciplinary tactics by type of toddler noncompliance. *Parenting: Science & Practice, 18*, 141–171. doi:10.1080/15295192.2018.1465304

Larzelere, R. E., Lin, H., Payton, M. E., & Washburn, I. J. (2018c). Longitudinal biases against corrective actions. *Archives of Scientific Psychology, 6*, 243–250. doi:10.1037/arc0000052

Larzelere, R. E., Morris, A. S., & Harrist, A. W. (Eds.). (2013). *Authoritative Parenting: Synthesizing Nurturance and Discipline for Optimal Child Development.* Washington, DC: American Psychological Association Press. http://www.apa.org/pubs/books/4318109.aspx

Larzelere, R. E., Trumbull, D. A., & Neiman, P. (2018d). Should pediatricians base their parenting advice on advocacy or science?: Comment on *Pediatrics, 142*(6), e20183112.

Lee, S., Grogan-Kaylor, A., & Berger, L. (2014). Parental spanking of 1-year-old children and subsequent child protective services involvement. *Child Abuse & Neglect, 38*(5), 875–883.

Lorber, M. F., O'Leary, S. G., & Smith Slep, A. M. (2011). An initial evaluation of the role of emotion and impulsivity in explaining racial/ethnic differences in the corporal punishment. *Developmental Psychology, 47*(6), 1744–1749.

McLoyd, V. C., Hardaway, C. R., & Jocson, R. M. (2019). *African American Parenting*. In Handbook of Parenting, Volume 4: Social Conditions and Applied Parenting Routledge Accessed on: 26 Aug 2019 https://www.routledgehandbooks.com/doi/10.4324/9780429398995-3

Mitchell, S. J., Lewin, A., Horn, I. B., Rasmussen, A., Sanders-Phillips, K., Valentine, D., & Joseph, J. G. (2009). Violence exposure and the association between young African American mothers' discipline and child problem behavior. *Academic Pediatrics, 9,* 157–163.

Nobles, W. W. (1974a). Africanity: Its role in Black families. *The Black Scholar, 5*(9), 10–17. doi:10.1080/00064246.1974.11431425

Peters, M. F. (1976). *Nine Black Families: A Study of Household Management and Child Rearing in Black Families with Working Mothers*. Unpublished doctoral dissertation, Harvard University.

Peters, M. F. (1985). Racial socialization of young Black children. In H. McAdoo, & J. McAdoo (Eds.), *Black Children* (pp. 159–173). Beverly Hills: Sage.

Portes, P. R., Dunham, R. M., & Williams, S. (1986). Assessing child rearing style in ecological settings: Its relation to culture, social class, early age intervention and scholastic achievement. *Adolescence, 21*, 723–735.

Richman, S. B., & Mandara, J. (2013). Do socialization goals explain differences in parental control between Black and White parents? *Family Relations, 62*(4), 625–636.

Roberts, D. (2012). Prison, foster care, and the systemic punishment of Black mothers. *UCLA Law Review, 59*, 1474–1504.

Roberts, D. (2011). Child protection as surveillance of African American families. *Journal of Social Welfare and Family Law, 36*(4), 426–437.

Roberts, D., & Sangoi, L. (2018). *Black Families Matter: How the Child Welfare System Punishes Poor Families of Color*. https://theappeal.org/black-families-matter-how-the-child-welfare-system-punishes-poor-families-of-color-33ad20e2882e/

Rohner, R. P., & Melendez-Rhodes, T. (2019). Perceived parental acceptance–rejection mediates or moderates the relation between corporal punishment and psychological adjustment: Comment on Gershoff et al. (2018). *American Psychologist, 74*(4), 500–502. https://doi.org/10.1037/amp0000437

Russell, J., & Cooper, T. (2011). *The NIS-4: What It All Means (And Doesn't Mean)*. National Council of Juvenile and Family Court Judges Permanency planning for children department.

Sandlowski, M. (2000). What ever happened to qualitative description? *Research in Nursing and Health, 23*, 334–340.

Sedlack, A. J., Mettenburg, J., Basena, M., Petta, I., McPherson, K., Greene, A., & Li, S. (2010). *Fourth National Incidence Study of Child Abuse and Neglect (NIS-4):*

Report to Congress, Executive Summary. Washington, DC: U. S. Department of Health and Human Services, Administration for Children and Families.

Sege, R., & Siegel, B. (2018). Effective Discipline to Raise Healthy Children. *Pediatrics, 142*(6), 1–10.

Thompson, R., Dancy, B., Wiley, L., Najdowski, T., Perry, R., Wallis, J., Mekawi, Y. & Knafl, K. (2013). African American Families' Expectations and Intentions for Mental Health Services. *Administration and Policy in Mental Health and Mental Health Services Research, 40*(5), 371–383.

Yoos, H. L., Kitzman, H., Olds, D. L., & Overacker, I. (1995). Child rearing beliefs in the African–American community: Implications for culturally competent pediatric care. *Journal of Pediatric Nursing, 10*(6), 343–352.

Chapter 1

Historical and Present Research on African American Child Discipline

Any examination of African American parenting must start with the fundamental premise that the African American family, including its definition, character, and child-rearing features, began in Africa and not in the United States (Nobles, 1974). In fact, the seminal work of Nobles (1974a,b, 1988), along with the writings of Billingsley (1968, 1992), Hill (1971), and Staples (1976), avow that the African American family is best understood as a system deriving its core values from its West African heritage. For example, in Yoruba thought (the Yoruba people are one of the largest indigenous groups in Africa), the concept of Omoluwabi (a good person) is definitive in terms of understanding the constitutive elements of a human being (Fayemi, 2009). These core characteristics include a strong valuing of children, respect for the elderly, recognition of the importance of purpose, spirituality, and extended family kinship, as well as responsibilities toward oneself and other people (Busari et al., 2017; Nobles, 1974, 1988; Okafor, 2003).

Historical and present writings have revealed that in many West African societies, it is the duty of parents and elders to cultivate these qualities in children (Ayokunle et al., 2013; Fadipe, 1970; Fayemi, 2009; Ogunnaike & Houser, 2002). For example, Okafor (2003) examined the child-rearing practices of rural families in Igbo-speaking Eastern Nigeria. The study utilized a focus group method to interview 400 men and women from 20 different villages. All members of the research team spoke Ibo. The findings revealed that children were taught by their parents to respect the values and beliefs transmitted from their ancestors. Particularly, children were taught not to look older people straight in the eye, and that they should only speak when they are spoken to. Parents used disciplinary methods such as spanking and denial of playtime in order to enforce appropriate behaviors. Some studies highlighted the performance of errands as a way for parents to foster key attributes in their children such as responsibility, obedience, and respect for elders.

Akinware et al. (1992) and Ogunnaike and Houser (2002) found in their studies of Yoruba child-rearing practices that the assignment of errands began as early as age two, and included tasks such as putting things away and fetching objects for their parents. As the children grew older, the errands advanced to tasks such as taking items to neighbors and buying items either from neighbors or area merchants. These tasks provided opportunities for children to learn about the environment, elements of communication with others, and to learn how to be dependable. Social scientists have maintained that African core values and child-rearing practices were not severed by the atrocities of 246 years (1619–1865) of physical bondage in the United States, and that they should not be viewed as standards that all African American families adhere to or implement, but rather as thematic influences with varying degrees of saliency within families (Arnold, 2002; Noble, 1974).

However, it is important to recognize that ever since the first slave ship landed in the United States, African Americans have been placed outside the human family (Johnson, 2006). During slavery, the American slave code classified Black male and female slaves as animals or "chattel." For example, according to the 1853 Civil Code 229 in the State of South Carolina, "Slaves shall be deemed, sold, taken, reputed, and adjudged in law to be chattel personal, in the hands of their owners and possessors, executors and administrators" (Goodell, 1986, p. 23). In regards to female slaves, Wheeler's Law of Slavery, which was a document used by court judges to interpret all of the civil codes governing slavery, stated that "black female slaves are upon the same footing and to be awarded upon the same rules as other female animals" (Goodell, 1986, p. 85).

Probably the most compelling evidence of societal acceptance of the dehumanization of Blacks during slavery was the fact that the United States had over 500,000 Africans in chattel bondage when the Declaration of Independence was signed (Dubois, 1909), which proclaimed at the time: "We hold these truths to be self-evident that all men are created equal, that are endowed by their Creator with certain unalienable Rights, that among these are Life, Liberty and the Pursuit of Happiness" (Declaration of Independence, 1776). It is the privilege of "liberty," namely the right for African Americans to parent children, that is critical for this discussion (Herbert, 2005).

During the nineteenth century, laws were developed that established the family as an autonomous unit and established the framework for the public governance of private life that remains today (Burnham, 1987). However, slave families were not recognized by family law. Each slave (mother, father, or child) stood as an individual unit of property who could be sold by the slave owner at any time. In fact, DuBois (1909), who is credited for writing the first book on African American family life, stated that a "slave has no more legal authority over his child than a cow has over her calf" (p. 22). Further, legal scholar Burnham (1987) contends that family law declared slave mothers and fathers to be "a different kind of human being . . . too dumb and childish to themselves parent (therefore incapable of child rearing), and sexually licentious (therefore unsuited to marriage and family bonds)" (p. 189).

Despite this dehumanizing situation, African American parents defied the efforts of slave owners to destroy the integrity of African American families. Prominent historian Franklin (1997, 2000) has cited numerous examples of slaves running away from their plantations, risking their lives in search of their children. Additionally, historical data, such as plantation documents and interviews with former slaves, have confirmed that African American parents provided a sense of security for family members and properly carried out the task of socializing their children (Billingsley, 1992; Jenkins, 1995; Schwartz, 2000).

It is important to note that much of the discussion regarding African American family life during slavery is centered on extended family and "kin" relationships, and that mothers and fathers exerted little influence in the raising of their children (Schwartz, 2000). However, researchers are quick to point out that although the threat of being sold by slave owners was always present for African American families, the extended family network did not supersede distinct parenting rules, goals, and aspirations that mothers and fathers had for their children (Gutman, 1977; Sudarkasa, 1997). Furthermore, in their attempts to shape the lives of their children according to their own morals and values, slave parents created a world of their own that refuted the belief that they or their children were somehow subhuman. Often, the principles of God and how humans were defined by God nullified what slave owners said and became the primary component of parenting in terms of defining the identities of children (Blassingame, 1972; Moody, 2001; Schwartz, 2000). It is also worthy to note that the lessons that slave children learned from their parents about obedience were complex. According to his systematic review of letters and interviews of former slaves, Blassingame (1972) noticed that slave parents taught children obedience as a means of avoiding suffering or death by the slave owner. Simultaneously, children were often instructed to fight their masters and overseers in order to protect their relatives. Within the slave community, authority over children was vested in parents, and when a death or a slave trade disrupted the family, other slaves assumed parental authority roles in place of the child's real mother and father (Blassingame, 1972; Gutman, 1977; Sudarkasa, 1997).

HISTORICAL PERSPECTIVES ON CHILD
DISCIPLINE POST-SLAVERY

In considering a discussion of disciplinary practices within African American families post-slavery, it is necessary to understand the history of child discipline in the United States. This brief review is by no means exhaustive, and several perspectives may have been updated or extended. Rather, this discussion acknowledges that today's recommended child disciplinary approaches have not occurred in a vacuum, but rather are built upon several traditional psychological concepts. A survey of the literature indicates that prior to the twentieth century, middle-class Protestant mothers were the most influential in guiding the practice of child discipline in American homes. Moreover, the ideas of child rearing were mainly provided by White American middle-class and upper-middle-class mothers who published their advice in the books, magazines, and newspapers of that period. Most writers of that time advocated for physical discipline and unquestioned obedience alongside love for the child (Langdon & Stout, 1952; Miller & Swanson, 1958).

The beginning of the twentieth century marked a significant shift in the relations between parents and their children. A child psychiatrist named Alfred Adler who lived and worked in Vienna, Austria, introduced a democratic approach to discipline to the field of family counseling. Adler believed that most problems that parents and children had were a direct outgrowth of their poor relationships with one another (Adler, 1930). He attributed the disintegration of the family at the beginning of the twentieth century as a direct result of a changing society, one which was moving away from a traditional, autocratic posture toward something more democratic, with equal rights for men and women, as well as children. Furthermore, he felt that the traditional methods of rearing children had become outdated and ineffective as society became more democratic.

Rudolf Dreikurs (1964, 1968) extended and popularized Adler's ideas in the United States by applying his principles to the discourse of child misbehavior and discipline. Since the Adlerian philosophy rests on the assumption of a democratic family atmosphere, Dreikurs challenged the arbitrary use of punishment (spanking, withdrawal of privileges, etc.) and rewards by parents as stimulants for behavior change in children. He contends that:

> No amount of punishment will bring about lasting submission. At best, parents gain only temporary results from punishment. When the same punishment has to be repeated again and again, it should be obvious it does not work. (Dreikurs, 1968, p. 69)

Instead, Dreikurs believed that the most effective means of discipline was the use of democratic, empowering methods such as natural and logical consequences which allowed children to experience the consequences of their own actions. From an Adlerian perspective, misbehaving children are discouraged children, so Dreikurs believed that encouragement was also essential in improving and maintaining appropriate behavior in children (Dreikurs, 1964, 1968).

Another perspective closely associated with the Adlerian democratic model of discipline is the person-centered viewpoint. Based on the fundamental principles of person-centered therapy, Thomas Gordon, the originator of Parent Effectiveness Training (PET), developed an alternative method of discipline that directly involved children in the process of determining the rules that they must follow (Gordon, 1970, 1988). Gordon (1970) believed that children would be more motivated to comply with rules or limits if they are given the opportunity to participate in determining what they should be. Like the Adlerian, Gordon also believed that the use of punishment and rewards were ineffective in terms of stimulating behavioral change in children. According to Gordon:

> Praise and other rewards heighten rivalries and competitiveness between children . . . For punishment to work, it must be severe, and yet when it is severe, youngsters look for all kinds of ways to avoid it, postpone it, weaken it, avert it, escape from it. They lie, put the blame on someone else, tattle, hide, plead for mercy and make promises to "never do it again." (Gordon, 1988, p. 70)

Alternatively, Gordon postulated that parents would more effectively influence the behavior of their children by using person-centered techniques, such as active listening and the use of "I" statements instead of "you" statements (Gordon, 1970, 1988).

In contrast to the person-centered and Adlerian perspectives are the ideas and principles of the behavioral viewpoint. Moreover, Skinner (1976), the originator of behavior modification, contended that behaviors that are reinforced tend to be repeated, and those that are discouraged tend to be extinguished.

> A positive reinforcer strengthens any behavior that produces it: a glass of water is positively reinforcing when we are thirsty, and if we then draw and drink a glass of water, we are more likely to do so again on similar occasions. A negative reinforcer strengthens any behavior that reduces or terminates it: when we take off a shoe that is pinching we are more likely to do so again when a shoe pinches. (Skinner, 1976, p. 51)

However, Bandura (1977), the creator of the Social Learning Theory, maintained the perspective that people were not buffeted by environmental stimuli. Instead, he assumed that people learned from each other, via observation, imitation, and modeling.

The capacity to use symbols provides humans with a powerful means of dealing with their environment. Through verbal and imagined symbols people
process and preserve experiences in representational forms that serve as guides
for future behavior. The capability for intentional action is rooted in symbolic
activities. Images of desirable futures foster courses of action designed to lead
toward more distant goals. (p. 13)

From a social learning perspective, aggressive behavior in children is primarily
a product of problematic (poor modeling) and inconsistent parenting. This conflicting and harsh discipline may make it difficult for children to foresee what
kind of reaction is likely to be witnessed based on their own conduct (Bandura
& Walters, 1959; Bandura, 1977; Patterson et al., 1989). Nationally recognized
parenting programs such as *Incredible Years*, *Strengthening Families Program*,
and *Strong African American Families Program* are influenced by Gerald
Patterson's and Albert Bandura's theoretical views on parenting behavior.

   Another perspective on parental disciplinary styles is offered by the seminal work of Baumrind (1966, 1972). She identified three prototypes of adult
control: (a) *authoritarian*, which is a high degree of parental control stressing
obedience, punitive disciplinary measures, and involves little verbal interaction between parent and child; (b) *authoritative*, defined as rational control
over children's behavior stressing autonomy, disciplined conformity, verbal
give and take between parent and child, and the preference to employ reason;
and (c) *permissive*, defined as a non-punitive and non-restrictive approach
toward the child's behavior, in which there is low control and power exercised over the child.

   In her initial studies of the effect of parental control on child behavior,
Baumrind (1966) linked authoritarian parenting practices to children who
were discontented, withdrawn, and distrustful, and conversely linked authoritative parenting practices to children who were self-reliant, self-controlled,
explorative, and content. However, when Baumrind (1972) separately analyzed the data that she had gathered on sixteen African American children
and their families, she found that "unlike their White counterparts, the most
authoritarian of these families produced the most self-assertive and independent girls" (p. 261). Baumrind concluded that if African American families
were viewed by White norms, they appeared authoritarian, but that, unlike
their White counterparts, the most authoritarian of these families actually
produced girls with outstanding competencies (Baumrind, 1972).

   It is important to highlight the fact that the traditional theories and concepts that dominate the child discipline literature undertake a universal norm
of parenting conduct. That is, the presumptions made by White American/
European theorists with respect to problematic parent behaviors, harsh discipline, and intentionality are applicable and generalizable to African American

parents. Further, according to prominent African American philosopher Yancy (2002), this exclusionary practice involves a form of erasure. African American parents are denied the status of being agents of their own lives, and their worldview is denied any sense of authority. It should be noted that several current parenting initiatives (e.g., Incredible Years, Incredible Years, Strengthening Families Program, and Strong African American Families Programs) have created or adapted their curriculums to meet the "cultural" needs of their participants. Notwithstanding, these programs still leave unproblematized their assumptions concerning child discipline and explanations for child misbehavior.

The historical absence of an African American viewpoint regarding the fundamental ways that parents raise children is not because of benign neglect within the social science field. For example, both McLoyd (2006) and Cicchetti et al. (2013) have evaluated the experiences of African Americans scholars and the treatment of African American children and families in child development research. They noticed the difficulty African American scholars faced when attempting to secure funding for their research and being able to publish their findings in mainstream journals. The authors also highlighted a lack diversity of the research participants upon which normal processes of child development are documented, while African American youth behaviors are characterized in a pathological manner.

Regarding African American families, many African American scholars (e.g., Billingsley, 1969; Hill, 1971; Peters, 1976, 1985; Taylor, 1991) have cited several methodological, analytical, and interpretative weaknesses to previous investigations of African American parenting practices. For example, Peters (1976, 1985) and Taylor (1991), who conducted extensive reviews of parent–child studies in the social science literature, found that when the research population involved both White American and African American parents, mainstream child-rearing practices were held as the standard; however, if White American parents were not part of the study, African American parents' child-rearing standards were compared to White American mainstream standards indirectly and by assumption. In either case, parenting behaviors that deviated from the mainstream approach to child rearing were viewed as inferior and problematic (Blau, 1981; Portes et al., 1986; Radin & Kamii, 1965).

AFRICAN AMERICAN PARENTING: A FOCUS ON CHILD DISCIPLINE

Before surveying the existing research that details the disciplinary practices of African American parents, it is important to recognize earlier writings and research that analyzed the African American family within context. In 1909, W. E. B. Dubois published the first evaluation of the African American family experience. His study utilized census data and government reports, along with a detailed study of thirteen African American households, to describe daily issues such as marriage, spending on basic needs, and the emergence of stable families (Dubois, 1909; Stewart, 1990). However, Frazier (1939) is credited for conducting the first systematic study of African American families, contending that the behaviors of parents were primarily shaped by the institution of slavery. Because plantation records and slave narratives affirmed the notion that slave mothers were often required to nurse the slave master's children and to work tirelessly in the field immediately after childbirth, Frazier questioned the ability of slave mothers to be nurturing parents to their children.

Frazier's (1959) research also addressed the social conditions of African American mothers and fathers post-slavery and during their migrations to the North. He reported that many African American fathers had deserted their families, and that African American mothers worked full-time jobs. However, Frazier was quick to point out that the "desertion" on the part of the father was primarily because of employment reasons (unable to find work in the local area), and that mothers had to work because of the poverty status of most African American families during that time. However, he concluded that the inadequacy of this type of family structure was the cause of much juvenile delinquency in the African American community.

The details of Frazier's seminal work regarding African American parenting are important because of its influence on the development of social policy to address the "negro problem" in the United States during the 1950s and 1960s. Specifically, in 1965, Senator Daniel Moynihan, using Frazier's thesis regarding the disorganization of the African American unit, believed that the African American family structure was pathological, and that African American children would have to "escape" from their parents and learn from the society at large how to become functional citizens (Rainwater & Yancey, 1967). The report, which focused on 25 percent of African American homes, primarily low income, concluded that if African American children remained with their parents, their lives would lead to juvenile delinquency and adult criminality. As a result, Moynihan declared that a national initiative be instituted in order to help African American parents rear their children like other families (Rainwater & Yancey, 1967).

Consequently, African American scholars challenged the pejorative nature of Moynihan's national agenda by illuminating the strengths and viability of the Black family. Specifically, Billingsley (1968) pointed out that conditions hindering Black families have commonly afflicted other American families as well. He emphasized that none of these factors affect all or even the majority of African American families. Moreover, Hill (1993) identified the strengths that facilitate the ability of African American families to meet the needs of its members. Factors such as strong kinship bonds, strong work orientation, adaptability of family roles, strong achievement orientation, and strong religious orientation have been central to the historical and present core of African American families. Nonetheless, the controversial Moynihan report spawned three decades of research focused on African American parents changing their child-rearing practices. Most notable were social scientists' preoccupations with the disciplinary styles of African American parents. The basis for this attention was attributed to a significant amount of research studies and writings that consistently found that African American mothers used physical punishment or other perceived negative parenting strategies (e.g., order child not to) more than White American mothers.

As a result, several prominent studies have attempted to expand the understanding of child discipline within African American culture by focusing on the interpersonal, social, and cultural aspects of discipline within African American families. Peters (1976) observed, and recorded in detail for nine months, the disciplinary behaviors of nine working-class African American families, and reported that mothers expected their children to be "courteous and respectful to adults," "honest and truthful," and "curious and eager to learn," (p. 148) and described their disciplinary practices as "no-nonsense" parenting. They also wanted children to display good manners (e.g., saying "yes, ma'am," and "no, sir," etc.) toward adults. An indication of disrespect was "talking back" (to answer a parent in a rude or defiant tone, or to respond to a parent when a child is expected to remain silent). One parent stated that "it is just as bad as lying." Disrespect is also demonstrated by the constant interruption of parental conversation. Parents considered talking back to be a serious behavioral problem. Peters also chronicled the following behaviors in Table 1.1 that "bothered" mothers, and their disciplinary response to each transgression.

Staples (1976, 1993) investigated African American households and found that parents expect a set standard of conduct, believe in forceful compliance when necessary, and have few "give and take" discussions. Staples also noted that, though African American parents disciplined with the liberal use of the rod, African American children are raised in an "anxiety-free" upbringing, with a great deal of love and support.

Barnes (1985) illuminated the parenting practices of middle-class African Americans, conducting an exploratory study of thirty-five African American middle-class families. For ten months, Barnes interacted in the homes, churches, and communities of the residents of Golden Towers, an African American middle-class neighborhood. Her study revealed that the women in Golden Towers assumed the major responsibility for disciplining their children, but that the mothers felt that men were more effective disciplinarians.

Table 1.1   What Bothers Some Mothers versus What Mothers Do

What Bothers Some Mothers	What Mothers Do
"Having to have the last word." (daughter, age eight)	"We have conversations about it daily."
"When they fight." (children ages four to nine)	"I talk to them about it."
"Being destructive." (son, age four)	"I spank him for it."
"Telling them to do something, and they pout or go stomping about." (children ages fiveseven)	"I yell at them to stop."
"Sits on it when I tell her to do something." (daughter, age eight)	"I speak twice. If they don't hear the first two, I let them feel it."
"Talking back." (all ages)	"If it gets out of hand, I resort to higher means."
"Not cleaning up the mess in their room." (children, ages five to eight)	"When it goes too far, I've got a plastic rope I can use."
"Being fresh." (child, age four)	"I make her go sit in her chair."

Created by Author.

Barnes also noted that both parents utilized several types of discipline, including confinement to rooms, closets, or corners, and the denial of privileges. Spanking was another method used to discipline children.

Denby and Alford (1996), in their qualitative study of African American disciplinary styles, also reported child conduct that often warranted firm discipline. For example, participants identified "having to repeat the same thing over and over again," "when explanations don't get through to the child," and "if a child's behavior would place him or her in danger" as problematic behaviors. Parents in this study discussed problematic behavior with their children and used clear commands and the withdrawal of privileges in order to address misbehavior. Physical discipline, if used, was accompanied by an explanation for its use.

Similarly, in my 1998 investigation of 121 African American parents, I found that participants frequently discussed problematic behaviors with their children. African American mothers and fathers employed less coercive disciplinary techniques for mild contextual situations, slightly more coercive techniques for moderate contextual situations, and reserved the most coercive techniques for severe contextual situations. The age of the child was a significant factor for moderate and severe contextual situations. More recent studies (Adkison-Bradley, 2014; Brodosky & DeVet, 2000; Horn et al., 2004; Greene & Garner, 2012; Mitchell et al., 2009) also confirmed the finding that African American parents preferred verbal discussion in addressing problematic behaviors with their children, and only used physical discipline as a last resort.

RACIAL SOCIALIZATION

An important issue that influences the disciplinary practices of African American mothers and fathers is the role of racial socialization. African American parents have the unique task of preparing their children to thrive in a society that has been historically racist toward them, in a process known as "racial socialization" (Stevenson & Davis, 1994). Dr. Howard Stevenson, a professor at the University of Pennsylvania, has extensively researched the concept of *racial socialization*, which he defines as the process of communicating messages and behaviors to children in order to bolster their sense of identity, given the reality that their life experiences may include racially hostile encounters (Stevenson, 1995; Stevenson et al., 2001). He identified the following assumptions in considering the relevance of racial socialization in the lives of children and families:

(1) That one cannot underestimate the influence of direct and indirect messages on self-esteem and its multiple components (e.g., personal, racial, gender).
(2) That racial tension is so basic a phenomenon in American society that it cannot be avoided, no matter how educated, sophisticated, or wealthy one might become.
(3) Seemingly minor or peripheral issues regarding cultural identity development vary in importance among a diverse group of Americans. (p. 357).

As early as preschool, African American children are bombarded with negative messages about race (Tatum, 1997). African American parents often transmit messages about racial and individual pride, expectations of discrimination, and intercultural relations to their children (McNeil et. al., 2014; Stevenson, 1994). African American parents also routinely engage in racial socialization practices as part of normal parenting activities (Coard et al., 2004). Moreover, Denby and Alford (1996), in their study of African American parenting styles, identified four primary goals of discipline related to socializing African American children about race. The goals are to teach African American children (1) about situations they may encounter that relate to racial differences; (2) that they must work extra hard because discrimination against African Americans is so prevalent in society; (3) that life is not fair, especially for African Americans; and (4) that children must know survival techniques as they relate to race differentials.

Although there have been many recent studies exploring the breadth and depth of racial and ethnic socialization in African American families, I wanted to highlight the original thinking and core assumptions of the racial socialization concept, as this perspective has had a major influence on my work with African American parents. You will notice throughout this book that I do not specifically discuss my child discipline findings comparable to

the actual verbal messages conveyed by parents. These messages and/or practices were embedded or assumed by many African American mothers and
fathers who participated in my current and previous studies, and this racial
child-rearing reality provides a foundational context for understanding the
phenomenon of child discipline in African American homes.

REFERENCES

Ackerman, A. M. (2017). An integrated model for counselor social justice advocacy
   in child welfare. *The Family Journal: Counseling and Therapy for Couples and
   Families*, 25(4), 1–9.
Adkison-Bradley, C. (2011). Seeing African Americans as competent parents:
   Implications for family counselors. *The Family Journal, 19*, 307–313.
Adkison-Bradley, C., Terpstra, J., & Dormitorio, B. (2014). Child discipline in
   African American families: A study of patterns and context. *The Family Journal,
   22*, 198–205.
Adkison-Johnson, C., & Johnson, P. (2019). Counseling people of the African
   Diaspora in the United States. In. C. Lee (Eds.), *Multicultural Issues in
   Counseling: New Approaches to Diversity* (pp. 47–60). Alexandria, VA: The
   American Counseling Association.
Adkison-Johnson, C., Terpstra, J., Burgos, J., & Payne, D. (2016). African American
   child discipline: Differences between mothers and fathers. *Family Court Review,
   54*(2), 203–220.
Adler, A. (1930). *Guiding the Child: On the Principles of Individual Psychology*.
   New York: Greenberg Press.
Akinware, M.,Wilson-Oyelaran, E. B., Lapido, P. A., Pierce, D. A., and Zeitlin, M.
   F. (1992). *Child Care and Development in Nigeria: A Profile of Five UNICEF-
   Assisted LGAs*. Lagos: UNICEF.
Ayokunle, A. M., Wuraola, A. G., & Obuchi, D. (2013). Influence of socio-cultural
   factors on child's upbringing in Oshodi/Isolo local government area of Lagos state,
   Nigeria. *Ife PsychologIA, 21*(1), 206–216.
Bandura, A. (1977). *Social Learning Theory*. Englewood Cliffs, NJ: Prentice-Hall.
Bandura, A., & Walters, R. H. (1959). *Adolescent Aggression*. New York: The
   Ronald Press Company.
Barnes, A. S. (1985). *The Black Middle Class Family*. Bristol, IN: Wyndham Hall
   Press.
Baumrind, D. (1966). Effects of authoritative parental control on child behavior.
   Child Development, 37(4), 887–907.
Baumrind, D. (1972). An exploratory study of socialization effects on black children:
   Some black-white comparisons. *Child Development, 43*, 261–267.
Belgrave, F. Z., & Allison, K. W. (2014). *African American Psychology: From Africa
   to America*. Thousand Oaks: Sage Publication.
Billingsley, A. (1968). *Black Families in White America*. Englewood Cliffs, NJ:
   Prentice-Hall.

Billingsley, A. (1992). *Climbing Jacob's Ladder: The Enduring Legacy of African–American Families.* New York: Simon & Schuster.

Blassingame, J. W. (1972). *The Slave Community: Plantation Life in the Antebellum South.* New York, NY: Oxford University Press.

Blau, Z. S. (1981). *Black Children/ White Children: Competence, Socialization and Social Structure.* New York: The Free Press.

Boyd-Franklin, N. (2003). *Black Families in Therapy: Understanding the African American Experience.* New York, NY: Guilford Press.

Boyd-Franklin, N., & Bry, B. H. (2000). *Reaching Out in Family Therapy.* New York: The Guilford Press.

Boyd-Franklin, N., Cleek, E. N., Wofsy, M., & Mundy, B. (2013). *Therapy in the Real World: Effective Treatments for Challenging Problems.* New York: The Guilford Press.

Bradley, C. R. (1998). Child rearing in African American families: A study of disciplinary methods used by African American parents. *Journal of Multicultural Counseling and Development, 26,* 273–281.

Bradley, C. R. (2000). The disciplinary practices of African American fathers: A closer look. *Journal of African American Men, 5,* 43–61.

Brodsky, A. E., & De Vet, K. A. (2000). You have to be real strong: Parenting goals and strategies of resilient, urban, African American, single mothers. *Journal of Prevention and Intervention in the Community, 20*(1–2), 157–178.

Burnham, M. A. (1987). An impossible marriage: Slave law and family law. *Law and Inequality: Journal of Theory and Practice, 5*(2), 187–226.

Busari, D. A., Owojuyigbe, M. A., Okunola, R. A., & Mekoa, I. (2017). Cultural concepts employed in child discipline within rural Yoruba households: The Ayetoro-Oke African community. *Rural Society, 26*(2), 161–177.

Cicchetti, D., Spencer, M., & Swanson, D. (2013). Opportunities and challenges to the development of health children and youth living in diverse communities. *Development & Psychopathology, 25*(4pt2), 1551–1566.

Coard, S. I., Foy-Watson, S., Zimmer, C., & Wallace, A. (2007). Considering culturally relevant parenting practices in intervention development and adaptation: A randomized controlled trial of the Black Parenting Strengths and Strategies (BPSS) Program. *The Counseling Psychologist, 35*(6), 797–820. doi:10.1177/0011000007304592.

Denby, R. W., & Alford, K. A. (1996). Understanding African American discipline styles: Suggestions for effective social work intervention. *Journal of Multicultural Social Work, 4,* 81–98.

Doyle, O., Clark, T., Cryer-Coupet, Q., Nebbitt, V., Goldston, D., Estroff, S., & Magan, I. (2015). Unheard voices: African American fathers speak about their parenting practices. *Psychology of Men & Masculinity, 16*(3), 274–283.

Doyle, O., Estroff, S., Goldston, D., Dzirasa, E., Fontes, M., & Burriss, A. (2014). "You gotta have a good help mate": African American fathers' co-parenting experiences. *Psychology of Men & Masculinity, 15*(4), 377–386.

Doyle, O., Magan, I., Cryer-Coupet, Q., Goldston, D., & Estroff, S. (2016). "Don't wait for it to rain to buy an umbrella": The transmission of values from African American fathers to sons. *Psychology of Men & Masculinity, 17*(4), 309.

Dreikurs, R. (1964). *Children: The Challenge*. New York, NY: E.P. Dutton.

Dreikurs, R. (1968). *Logical Consequences*. New York: Van Rees Press.

DuBois, W. E. B. (1909). *The Negro American Family*. Cambridge: The M.I.T. Press.

Evans, H., & Fargason, C. (1998). Pediatric discourse on corporal punishment: A historical review. *Aggression and Violent Behavior, 3*(4), 357.

Fadipe, N. A. (1970). *The Sociology of the Yoruba*. Ibadan: Ibadan University Press.

Fayemi, A. K. (2009). Human personality and the Yoruba worldview: An ethico-sociological interpretation. *The Journal of Pan African Studies, 2*(9), 166–176.

Franklin, J. H. (1997). African American families: A historical note. In H. M. McAdoo (Ed.), *Black Families* (pp. 5–8).Thousand Oaks: Sage.

Franklin, J. H. (2000). *From Slavery to Freedom: The History of Negro Americans*. New York, NY: Knopf.

Frazier, E. F. (1939). *The Negro Family in the United States*. Chicago, IL: The University of Chicago Press.

Frazier, E. F. (1959). The Negro family in America. In R. N. Anshen (Ed.), *The Family: Its Function and Destiny* (pp. 65–84). New York: Harper & Row.

Goodell, W. (1986). *The American Slave Code* (Reprint). New York, NY: Negro University Press.

Gordan, T. (1970). *Parent Effectiveness Training*. New York: Wyden.

Gordan, T. (1988). Effectiveness training. *Person Centered Approach, 3*, 59–85.

Greene, K., & Garner, P. (2012). African American mothers' disciplinary responses: Associations with family background characteristics, maternal childrearing attitudes, and child manageability. *Journal of Family Economic Issues, 33*, 400–409.

Gutman, H. G. (1977). *The Black Family in Slavery and Freedom 1725–1925*. New York, NY: Vintage Books.

Hawkins, N. E., & Biglan, A. (1981). Paretning Skills. In J. L. Shelton (Ed.), *Behavioral Assignments and Treatment Compliance* (pp. 331–356). Champain, IL: Research Press.

Herbert, L. (2005). Plantation lullabies: How fourth amendment policing violates the fourteenth amendment right of African Americans to parent. *Journal of Civil Rights and Economic Development, 19*(2), 197–235.

Hill, R. (1972). *The Strengths of Black Families*. New York: Gardner Press.

Hill, R. (2004). *Black Overrepresentation: Synthesis of Research Findings*. Presentation to the Michigan advisory committee on the overrepresentation of children of color in child welfare.

Hill, R. B. (2006). *Synthesis of Research on Disproportionality in Child Welfare: An Update*. Washington, DC: The Casey-CSSP Alliance for Racial Equity.

Hines, P. M., & Boyd-Franklin, N. (2005). African American families. In M. McGoldrick, Giordano, J., & Garcia-Preto, N. (Eds.), *Ethnicity and Family Therapy* (pp. 87–100). NY: The Guildford Press.

Horn, I. B., Joseph, J. G., & Cheng, T. L. (2004). Nonabusive physical punishment and chld behavior among African American children: A systematic review. *Journal of the National Medical Association, 96*(9), 1162–1168.

Hrabowski, F. A., Maton, K. I., & Greif, G. L. (1998). *Beating the Odds: Raising Academically Successful African American Males*. New York, NY: Oxford University Press.

Jenkins, A. H. (1995). *Psychology and African Americans: A Humanistic Approach* (2nd ed.). Needham Heights: Allyn & Bacon.

Johnson, P. D. (2006). Counseling Black men: A contextualized humanistic approach. *Counseling and Values, 50,* 187–196. doi:10.1002/j.2161-007X.2006.tb00055.x

Johnson, P. D. (2016). Somebodiness and its meaning to African American men. *Journal of Counseling and Development, 94,* 333–344.

Langdon, G., & Stout, I. W. (1952). *Discipline of Well Adjusted Children.* New York: John Day Company.

Liebert, R. M., & Spiegler, M. D. (1987). *Personality: Strategies and Issues.* Chicago, IL: The Dorsey Press.

McLoyd, V. C. (2006). Our children too: A history of the first 25 years of the black caucus of the society for research in child development, 1973–1997: XI. the role of African American scholars in research on African American children: Historical perspectives and personal reflections. *Monographs of the Society for Research in Child Development, 71*(1), 121–144. Retrieved from http://libproxy.library.wmich.edu/login?url=https://search.proquest.com/docview/837457076?accountid=15099

McLoyd, V., & Randolph, S. (1986). Secular trends in the study of Afro-American children: A review of Child Development, 1936–1980. *Monographs of the Society for Research in Child Development, 50*(4–5), 78.

McNeil, S., Harris-McKoy, D., Brantely, C., Fincham, F., & Beach, S. R. (2014). Middle class African American mothers' depressive symptoms mediate perceived discrimination and reported child externalizing. *Journal of Child and Family Studies, 23,* 381–388. https://doi.org/10.007/s10826-013-9788-0.

Miller, D. R., & Swanson, G. E. (1958). *The Changing American Parent.* New York: John Wiley and Sons.

Mitchell, S. J., Lewin, A., Horn, I. B., Rasmussen, A., Sanders-Phillips, K., Valentine, D., & Joseph, J. G. (2009). Violence exposure and the association between young African American mothers' discipline and child problem behavior. *Academic Pediatrics, 9,* 157–163.

Moody, J. (2001). *Sentimental Confessions: Spiritual Narratives of Nineteenth-Century African American Women.* Athens, GA: The University of Georgia Press.

Nobles, W. W. (1972). African Philosophy: Foundations for Black Psychology. In Reginald Jones (Eds.), *Black Psychology* (pp 18–32). NY: Harper & Row.

Nobles, W. W. (1974a). Africanity: Its role in Black families. *The Black Scholar, 5*(9), 10–17. doi: 10. 1080/00064246.1974.11431425

Nobles, W. W. (1974b). African root and American fruit: The Black family. *The Journal of Social and Behavioral Sciences, 20,* 66–77.

Nobles, W. W. (1986). *Africanity and the Black Family: The Development of a Theoretical Model.* Oakland, CA: The Institute for He Advanced Study of Black Family Life and Culture.

Ogunnaike, O. A., & Houser, R. F. (2002). Yoruba toddlers' engagement in errands and cognitive performance on the Yoruba mental subscale. *International Journal of Behavioral Development, 26*(2), 145–153.

Okafor, C. B. (2003). Child rearing practices in Eastern Nigeria: Implications for social work in the United States. *International Journal of Global Health, 2*(2), 4–20.

Patterson, G. R., Debaryshe, B., & Ramsey, E. (1989). A developmental perspective on antisocial behavior. *American Psychologist, 44*(2), 329–335.

Peters, M. F. (1976). *Nine Black Families: A Study of Household Management and Child Rearing in Black Families with Working Mothers.* Unpublished doctoral dissertation, Harvard University.

Peters, M. F. (1985). Racial socialization of young Black children. In H. McAdoo, & J. McAdoo (Eds.), *Black Children* (pp. 159–173). Beverly Hills: Sage.

Portes, P. R., Dunham, R. M., & Williams, S. (1986). Assessing child-rearing style in ecological settings: Its relation to culture, social class, early age intervention and scholastic achievement. *Adolescence, 21*, 723–735.

Radin, N., & Kamii, C. (1965). The childrearing attitudes of disadvantaged Negro mothers and some educational implications. *Journal of Negro Education, 34*, 138–146.

Rainwater, L., & Yancey, W. L. (1967). *The Moynihan Report and the Politics of Controversy.* Cambridge: M.I.T. Press.

Schwartz, M. J. (2000). *Born in Bondage: Growing Up Enslaved in the Antebellum South.* Cambridge, MA: Harvard University Press.

Shelton, J. L., & Levy, R. L. (1981). *Behavioral Assignments and Treatment Compliance.* Champaign, IL: Research Press.

Skinner, B. F. (1976). *About Behaviorism.* New York: Vintage Books.

Staples, R. (1976). *Introduction to Black Sociology.* New York: McGraw Hill Book Company.

Staples, R. (1994). *Black Family: Essays and Studies* (5th ed.). New York: Van Nostrand Reinhold.

Stevenson, H. C., & Arrington, E. G. (2009). Racial/ethnic socialization mediates perceived racism and identity experiences of African American students. *Cultural Diversity and Ethnic Mental Health, 15*(2), 125–136.

Stevenson, H. C., & Davis, G. Y. (2004). Racial socialization. In R. J. (Eds), *Black Psychology* (pp. 353–381). Hampton, VA: Cobb and Henry Publishers.

Stevenson, H. C., Davis, G., & Abdul-Kabir, S. (2001). *Stickin" to, Watchn" Over, and Getting' With: An African American Parent's Guide to Discipline.* San Francisco: Josey Bass.

Stewart, J. B. (1990). Back to basics: The significance of Dubois's and Frazier's contributions for contemporary research on Black families. In Cheatham, H. E. & Stewart, J. B. (Eds.), *Black Families: Interdiscplinary Perspective* (pp. 5–27). New Brunswick: Transaction Publishers.

Sudarkasa, N. (1997). African American families and family values. In H. P. McAdoo (Ed.), *Black Families* (pp. 9–40). Thousand Oaks: Sage.

Taylor, R. (1991). Child rearing in African American families. In J. Everett (Ed.), *Child Welfare* (pp. 119–154). New Brunswick, NJ: Rutgers University Press.

Yancy, G. (2000). Feminism and the subtext of Whiteness: Black women's experiences as a site of identity formation and contestation of Whiteness. *The Western Journal of Black Studies, 24*, 156–166.

Chapter 2

Disciplinary Practices of African American Mothers

A discussion of the disciplinary styles of African American mothers is complex, because society has defined them in such restrictive and degrading ways (Roberts, 1997, 2002). Ever since the beginning of chattel slavery in the United States, African American women have been outside the typical American picture of motherhood (Hill-Collins, 2000). There are many stereotypical images and beliefs that society maintains of African American mothers. The depiction of African American mothers as feeble-minded, incompetent, lazy, reckless, and in need of supervision while attending to their children is embedded in the minds of many Americans. According to Roberts (1997), these "are also firmly held beliefs that represent and attempt to explain what we perceive to be the truth. They can become more credible than reality, holding fast even in the face of airtight statistics and rational argument to the contrary" (p. 23). In *Shattered Bonds: The Color of Child Welfare,* Roberts (2002) describes several controlling images of African American mothers that depict them as unfit to rear their children. For example, the neglectful, careless, and incompetent image of African American mothers stems from the portrait of the "Mammy" figure. According to Roberts (1997):

> The image of Mammy was based on the Black female house servant who cared for her master's children. Pictured as rotund and handkerchiefed, Mammy was both the perfect mother and the perfect slave: whites saw her as a passive nurturer, a mother figure who gave all without expectation of return, who not only acknowledged her inferiority to whites but who loved them. It is important to recognize, however, that Mammy did not reflect any virtue in Black motherhood. The ideology of Mammy placed no value on Black women as the mothers of their own children. Rather, whites claimed Mammy's total devotion to the master's children, without regard to the fate of Mammy's own offspring. What's

more, Mammy, while she cared for the master's children, remained under the constant supervision of her white mistress. She had no real authority over either the white children she raised or the Black children she bore. (p. 13)

Roberts (1997) also contended that White Americans believed that the supervision of African American mothers needed to continue after slavery:

Whites believed that Black mothers needed the moral guidance that slavery once afforded. Eleanor Tayleur, for example, argued that deprived of the intimate contact with their morally superior white mistresses, freed Black women displayed uncontrolled passion and ignorance. According to Tayleur, Black women exhibited a purely animal passion toward their children, which often led to horrible abuses . . . when they are little, she indulges them blindly when she is in good humor, and beats them cruelly when she is angry; and once past their childhood her affection for them appears to be exhausted. She exhibits none of the brooding mother-love and anxiety which the white woman sends after her children as long as they live. (p. 14)

While the Mammy image rendered African American mothers both incompetent and violent, the matriarch portrayal signified a reckless and aggressive African American mother. According to the groundbreaking work of Patricia Hill-Collins (2000):

The Black matriarchy thesis argued that African-American women who failed to fulfill their traditional "womanly" duties at home contributed to social problems in Black civil society (Moynihan, 1965). Spending too much time away from home, these working mothers ostensibly could not properly supervise their children and thus were a major contributing factor to their children's failure at school. As overly aggressive, unfeminine women, Black matriarchs allegedly emasculated their lovers and husbands. . . . From the dominant group's perspective, the matriarch represented a failed mammy, a negative stigma to be applied to African-American women who dared reject the image of the submissive, hardworking servant. (p. 75)

These two specific portrayals of African American mothering concretize the utilization of White American parenting standards in the evaluation of child discipline in African American homes. Even in the first national study of child rearing in the United States, every aspect of child rearing in African American homes was contrasted with the parenting practices of lower- and middle-class White American mothers (Anderson, 1936). The 1936 study was conducted by the White House Committee on Child Health and Protection, chaired by John E. Anderson, the past president of the

American Psychological Association (APA). Participants were 2,758 White American families and 202 African American families, and the mothers from both groups were primarily interviewed. In comparison to the disciplinary practices of White American mothers, the researchers reported that African American children were spanked more frequently at each age level. It is important to note that the researchers classified spanking as "one of the most universally condemned methods of punishment."

From that point forward, a vast majority of investigations (e.g., Batrz & Levine, 1978; Deater-Deckard et al., 1996; Durrent et al., 1975; Gershoff & Grogan-Kaylor, 2016; Gershoff et al., 2012; Portes et al., 1986) compared White American mothers with the practices used by African American mothers. However, a large portion of these investigations pinpoint whether or not mothers engage in spanking or any forms of physical discipline.

PHYSICAL DISCIPLINE

Physical discipline, or more specifically, spankings, by mothers in general and African American mothers in particular have dominated the parenting discourse in most helping professions. However, words or phrases such as "whuppins," "beat down," "getting popped," "beat that ass," and "whupped that butt," often used to describe physical discipline in African American communities, are often considered explosive to White American mental health clinicians and social workers who may be unfamiliar with these colloquial terms.

For academics, clinicians, and child welfare workers who declare that all forms of physical discipline are child abuse, or refer to parental use of physical discipline as "hitting children," in-depth conversations about whuppins or spankings are infrequent. Questions such as *why* and *how* physical discipline or any other disciplinary method is used in African American homes are rarely addressed in great detail. Greene and Garner (2012) argue that African American mothers may have different frames of reference for physical discipline which are more nuanced than simply having attitudes for or against it. All cultures have rules concerning appropriate and inappropriate conduct with children, but beliefs may vary widely on what behaviors warrant discipline, as well as the types of discipline that should be used (Budd et al., 2011).

A few different investigations over the past two decades have reported noteworthy findings regarding the disciplinary strategies used by African American mothers. For instance, one of the most cited research studies is the work of Deater-Deckard et al. (1996) who examined the use of physical discipline among African American and White American mothers of preschool-age children, as well as externalizing behaviors. *Externalizing behaviors* in this investigation is defined as specific, non-compliant, physically aggressive, defiant, and delinquent behaviors (e.g., bragging, boasting, being disobedient at home or school, getting into frequent fights, preferring being with older kids, talking too much, being unusually loud, and threatening other people) (Doyle & McCarty, 2001). The results indicated that African American children were more likely to receive physical discipline than their White counterparts. The interaction between the race of the mother and level of discipline was significant for externalizing child behaviors, in that physical discipline was associated with externalizing behavior problems for White American children. However, there was not a significant association between the experience of physical discipline and subsequent behavioral problems for African American children. Deater-Deckard and colleagues (1996) concluded that African American parents may administer physical discipline in an emotionally controlled, normative manner, and that African American children may not view their parents' use of physical discipline as representing a lack of warmth or concern for them.

McLoyd and Smith's (2002) examination of physical discipline and behavior problems in African American, European American, and Hispanic children also had noteworthy results. They found that through the span of multiple years, beginning when children were five years old, White American mothers increased their frequency of physical discipline use, whereas the frequency of use among African American mothers diminished over a similar timespan.

Lansford et al.'s (2004) longitudinal study of African American and White American adolescent externalizing behaviors showed that African American mothers used higher levels of physical discipline with their adolescent children than did White American mothers. However, the study also found that physical discipline was related to higher levels of resultant externalizing behaviors for White American adolescent children, but lower levels of externalizing behaviors for African American children.

Ispa and Halgunseth (2004), in their qualitative study of nine African American mothers, attempted to clarify the terms and behaviors associated with using physical punishment with preschoolers. Participants made it clear that "popping" and "tapping" referred to little slaps on the arm, hand, leg, or buttocks. The hand was the most frequently "popped" body part for toddlers. Mothers in the study used this technique for mild to moderate to serious misbehaviors (e.g., touching something fragile, ignoring a request to pick up toys, or inserting something into an electrical outlet) after repeated warnings were ignored. Whuppins, on the other hand, consisted of striking a child on the buttocks with an open hand, belt, or hairbrush. Whuppins were reserved for specific behaviors that involved breaking valued objects, putting younger siblings in danger, or showing disrespect (talking back to parents or grandparents, cussing, or repeatedly not listening to previously stated rules) to the mother or another adult. Similarly, a more recent study (Taylor et al., 2011) of African American mothers of elementary-age school children found that physical discipline was not the only method used, and that mothers used these techniques for infractions such as signs of disrespect when previous warnings had failed.

It is a prevalent view in the existing psychological literature that African American low-income mothers are the primary users of physical disciplinary practices in African American communities. However, Horn et al. (2004) found that the low-income and middle- to upper-income African American mothers were reasonably similar to one another with respect to disciplinary beliefs and practices. Moreover, when physical discipline was used, middle- to upper-income African American parents were bound to use an option other than a hand with which to spank their child. Overall, there was a greater endorsement of disciplinary methods such as teaching and the withdrawal of privileges. Substantial variability among middle-class African American mothers has also been noted in previous studies (Bluestone & Tamis-Lemonda, 1999; Bradley, 1998, 2000; Greene & Garner, 2012). It is important to note that African American mothers in the studies by Ispa and Halgunseth (2004), Taylor et al. (2010), and Greene and Garner (2012) were aware of the potential harm that could be caused to children if physical discipline was conducted recklessly, or was not handled in a controlled and strategic manner.

In my investigations of the child discipline methods of African American mothers, I found that "discuss matters with children," "given child warning look," and "order child not to do it again" were the most frequently used techniques for preschool- and elementary-age children (Bradley, 1998, 2000). Mothers used "discuss the matter" and "withdrawal of privileges" as the preferred strategies with their teenagers. Generally, mothers primarily used "demand child not to do it again" as the first response to misbehavior and a second response with which to address moderate disciplinary situations with their preschoolers. The mothers used more concrete methods than African American fathers with their adolescent children (Adkison-Johnson et al., 2016). They also intensified their disciplinary practices in addressing severe adolescent contextual situations. African American mothers use more intense disciplinary methods across most misbehavior situations compared to African American fathers, regardless of whether or not the mother was living with the father.

As mentioned in chapter 1, my most recent investigation spotlights how African American parents are currently thinking about child-rearing objectives and child behavior expectations. This chapter will present a small portion of the analysis of the interviews that identified disciplinary practices, concerns, and goals of African American mothers. The twenty-six African American women involved in this investigation were mothers of preschool (three to five), elementary (six to eleven), preadolescent (twelve to fourteen), and late adolescent (fifteen to seventeen) children. Participants comprised both one-parent and two-parent households. Family size ranged from one to four children, and children's ages ranged from two to seventeen. Most of the mothers had completed between some college and a college degree. The average household income level was $20,000–$39,999, with five mothers from household incomes of $80,000 and up. The mothers ranged in age from thirty-one to fifty-four ($M = 43$). Given the risk involved in discussing actual disciplinary practices and/or responses, names and titles have been replaced by pseudonyms. Quotes are presented in the vernacular in which they were spoken. Three themes were identified from the interviews: *These are the rules*, *Intentional and heartfelt discussions*, and *Rethinking discipline strategy*.

These Are the Rules

Establishing clear rules and reinforcing firmly established boundaries helped mothers to encourage formative achievements with their children while adjusting behavior. Jayla confirmed this position concerning her elementary- and adolescent-age children: "I tell them . . . you know the rules in the house. You're supposed to make sure your friends know the rules in the house. All of you all are supposed to honor the rules in this house, too, because you all know how we roll." Sade provides the context for her rule-setting:

> I know some parents who their kids say, "I don't want to eat anymore. I don't want it." And then they're going to get to dessert, and they let them. And it's like, "Okay, you know you're not establishing rules or boundaries," so I think it is not as much as "You can't get the dessert, but these are the rules." And if you establish those rules, it follows other things that you do in the family. So by letting them have free will, "I'm not going to eat this. I'm going to do what I want," that's going to lead into other areas."

Sade also described her behavior expectations when her preschool children are with her out in public:

> I mean, it's funny because people have always seen us at the store, and they're like, "Your kids are so well-behaved." It's like, they get the rundown before we get out the car. Before we get out the car it's like, "Stay with me," or "Hold on to the basket. Don't run ahead. Don't ask for nothing when you get in the store.

Don't fall. Don't cry. These are the rules. Okay?" So when they get out the car, they know it, that's it.

The rules reflected the mother's cultural values and her intention to transmit these values to her children (Skinner & McHale, 2016; Street et al., 2017). Specifically, the rules were an intricate parity of defining behavioral limits and establishing culturally normative child conduct and self-discipline, alongside providing safety for their children from the larger society. This is consistent with research that found that firm limits set by African American parents "facilitate children's socialization into society, coordinate their interaction, maintain social order, and reflect parents' role in the socialization process" (Smetana & Chuang, 2001, p. 193).

Nearly all of the mothers spoke explicitly about how children should display respectful comportment toward parents, and consequences when that instruction is disregarded. Esther describes in detail the behavioral expectation regarding communication with her children:

> My children know . . . they can't talk to me crazy. They can't yell at me. They can't roll their eyes or look at me crazy. They can't be nasty in their tone to me. They can't give me the silent treatment. If I speak to them, they have to respond . . . So, everything else comes to a stop. I then ask, why didn't you hear me speak to you? If I speak to you with words, then you respond with words. If I speak to you in a normal tone of voice, you don't get to speak back in a whisper because we're communicating. I am just very direct in addressing that . . . My 10-year-old daughter had an attitude because I would not let her go to a friend's house. I called her and she didn't answer me. I went to her room and asked her did you hear me call you . . . she said yes! I went and got my belt . . . whupped her butt and told her "don't you ever ignore me when I call you." We have not had a problem since then on that issue.

For the participants in this investigation, respect from children is perceived broadly to preclude overt expressions of opposition, such as rolling their eyes, sucking their teeth, or ignoring a parent's command. According to Boyd-Franklin and Bry (2000), African American mothers meet these distinct expressions with intense emotion and firm discipline. Esther's parenting encounter represented the reactions from almost all of the other participants in this study. Mothers thought carefully and strategically about the use of physical discipline, especially with a belt. They were keenly aware that the impact of the punishment depended on their household discipline program. That is, their disciplinary program was based on a continuum that included the establishment of appropriate guidelines for conduct, clear communication about consequences, and less restrictive disciplinary methods (e.g., discussion, warnings, withdrawal of privileges), with physical discipline used as a final resort if necessary.

In one particular situation, a mother directly confronted her preadolescent son who had challenged her authority. Gloria describes how she addressed his behavior while driving to an event:

> I'm driving . . . my boys start arguing with each other . . . And so I reached back, and I'm like, "You all need to, stop, I'm driving." My oldest teenager said they were too big for me to do something. I couldn't believe it. I pulled over. And I was like oh, you think you can whip me now because you got a little height on you, because he had a little growth spurt over the summer. So I think he was feeling himself, too. And I was like, "So that's what you want to do because we can get out and do this?" And then, they both got quiet . . . they didn't do anything.

According to Hardy and Laszloffy (2005), adolescents demonstrating rebellious behaviors can cause concern for many adults. This mother may have viewed her son's non-compliance as an immature, reckless attempt to undermine the hierarchical system within the family. Hardy and Laszloffy (2005) explain further:

> From the perspective of most adults, adolescents often exhibit bizarre vacillations between states of childlike innocence and adult sophistication-hence, a form of madness. Trapped somewhere between childhood and adulthood, adolescents frequently struggle to mediate their conflicting needs and desires. On the one hand, they crave to be free, independent, and self-sufficient young adults. On the other hand, they long for the safety and security typically associated with the world of childhood. The pressure and uncertainty that these competing needs create often lead to behaviors that seem quite maddening to adults. (p. 126)

Combined with teaching children to manage their emotions and to interact appropriately with their community in a society that perceives African American male youth as threatening, this mother's disciplinary reaction can be understood in context. Because Gloria's sons erroneously perceived her to no longer be a threat to them, she might have wanted to send her sons a clear message that she was still "in charge."

Intentional and Often Heartfelt Discussions as a Disciplinary Strategy

Beyond establishing and enforcing rules to meet their parenting goals, each mother shared at least one disciplinary situation that had required the use of teaching and reflection in order to modify child behavior. Willa describes her disciplinary conversation with her thirteen-year-old daughter as follows:

> My daughter—the way she speaks to me, you know for some reason she doesn't see how she's being disrespectful with her words. She feels like she is just expressing herself but I've been trying to explain to her for a long time . . . there's a way to express yourself without being disrespectful and that is what she needs to learn how to do. I told her, "You can't say it how you want to say it. You can express (your feelings) to me. I want you to tell me. But think about what you're going to say before you say it." She wants to compare me to her friends' mother. I told her, "I don't have to take care of your friends, your friends are not raised in my household. I've never taught you to be disrespectful and why are we starting right now? You don't do what other people do, you follow your own lead, that's what makes you a leader." Those are the things I try to express to her . . . And now, she's just like, "Okay, mom. I'll change my words." I just want her to know she can talk to me . . . but it's got to be respectful.

This strategy is congruent with the works of Brodsky and DeVet (2000) and Denby and Alford (1996), who found that severe disciplinary strategies were rarely used for the goal of teaching human and spiritual qualities. Rather, verbal and instructive strategies were used most often to transmit the idea of purpose and respect toward oneself and other people. This approach also helps children to become independent thinkers and to anticipate and solve problems on their own (Johnson & Stanford, 2002; Stevenson et al., 2002).

A few disciplinary circumstances involved mothers having agonizing conversations with their late adolescent-age daughters. Patrice describes a behavioral situation with her daughter regarding her dating a young man who engaged in criminal activity:

> So she would lie. Then I found out she was seeing him. And I said to her, "You know, there's consequences for your actions." I'm ready to snatch her soul out. So don't play with me. She did it (saw him) again. I said, "You are not respecting this house and most importantly yourself. You can do anything you put your mind to . . . You are smart . . . you'll be going to college next year. But you can't stay here anymore. I only have children that live in my house . . . not people who think they can make their own decisions. Now, you marinate on that a while." She decided not to live in my house anymore. I had to let her go. It hurt . . . but it was the right decision.

According to Richman and Mandara (2013), adolescence is the formative period during which children seek to be close to and independent from their families, and to develop a sense of individuality. The mothers in this study closely monitored their children's friends, as well as their children's academic progress and career development. This is consistent with previous studies that found that parents who are academically demanding use firmer disciplinary strategies (Richman & Mandara, 2013; Smetana & Chuang, 2001). Parents may also exert greater control as a way of ensuring their adolescents' safety (Smetana & Gaines, 1999). It is important to note that the African American mothers in this study reported frustration with regard to how to support their teenage daughters' need for independence while also keeping them safe and focused on their academic goals.

RETHINKING DISCIPLINE STRATEGY

There were some mothers who revisited and changed their disciplinary approach when they thought that it was no longer effective. Zola describes this occurrence with her ten-year-old son:

> I can't remember exactly what he did, but it warranted more than just taking something away. I said, "You know I'm gonna have to whup you." He said, "Yes." So, I spanked him. I stopped. He said, "Mom, that didn't even hurt." And he was just serious. He wasn't saying that to insult me. He was just like, "Mom, that didn't do it. Sorry." So I then said, "Well . . . look at you and look at me. If I wanted to hurt you, you don't think I could hurt you? I just wanted to change your direction. So, are you gonna change your direction or not?" He said, "Yes." All right, then. And that was when I made up my mind, I'm not gonna try that no more, because that's not gonna work.

Shaylah, the mother of an eight-year-old daughter, states that:

> So I have whupped her in the past. But she's getting to the point, and I'm getting to the point where I'm old, and she likes to run and hide under things. And I just don't have the energy for that. I'm a firm believer in trying to talk to her and explain to her why things are happening and the consequences that are going to happen behind it.

Annette, the mother of a sixteen-year-old son, shares the following:

> Well, I think I was inconsistent in how I disciplined. I should have checked his behavior a while ago. I didn't want to appear to be strict . . . Now he's constantly feeling like he's at the level of these teachers, or anybody who's supposed to be in authority. I find myself yelling all the time and nothing happens. I'm ready to try something different.

Parents are more likely to use severe disciplinary tactics when children are consistently non-compliant. But mothers in the present study realized that as their children became older, physical discipline for some of their children became less effective, or the mothers had less energy with which to carry out the task. Mothers frequently communicated being open and effectively searching for additional approaches in order to address their child's behavior from a cultural, spiritual, and educational viewpoint.

In summary, the research presented in this chapter showed that the disciplinary practices used by African American mothers are multidimensional. Focusing on the arbitrary use of physical discipline by African American mothers continues to perpetuate the erroneous narrative that African American women are feeble-minded, reckless, and that they use parenting methods that put African American children at risk of being abused. The findings from this chapter add an important corrective in seeing African American mothers as competent disciplinarians.

REFERENCES

Adkison-Johnson, C., Terpstra, J., Burgos, J., & Payne, D. (2016). African American child discipline: Differences between mothers and fathers. *Family Court Review, 54*(2), 203–220.

Anderson, J. E. (1936). *The Young Child in the Home*. White House Conference on Child Health and Protection, Committee on the Infant and Pre-school Child. New York: Appleton-Century.

Bartz, K. W., & Levine, E. S. (1978). Child rearing by Black parents: A description and comparison to Anglo and Chicano parents. *Journal of Marriage and the Family, 40*, 709–719.

Bluestone, C., & Tamis-Lemonda, C. (1999). Correlates of parenting styles in predominantly working- and middle-class African American mothers. *Journal of Marriage and Family, 61*(4), 881–893.

Boyd-Franklin, N. (2003). *Black Families in Therapy: Understanding the African American Experience*. New York, NY: Guilford Press.

Boyd-Franklin, N., & Bry, B. H. (2000). *Reaching Out in Family Therapy: Home-Based, School, and Community Interventions*. New York: The Guilford Press.

Bradley, C. R. (1998). Child rearing practices used by African American parents. *Journal of Multicultural Counseling and Development, 26*, 273–281.

Bradley, C. R. (2000). The disciplinary practices of African American fathers: A closer look. *Journal of African American Men, 5*, 43–61.

Brodsky, A. E., & DeVet, K. A. (2000). You have to be real strong: Parenting goals and strategies of resilient, urban, African American, single mothers. *Journal of Prevention and Intervention in the Community, 20*, 157–178.

Budd, K., Clark, J., & Connell, M. (2011). Evaluation of parenting capacity in child protection. New York: Oxford University Press.

Comer, J. P., & Poussaint, A. F. (1975). *Black Child Care*. New York, NY: Plume Publishing.

Deater-Deckard, K., Dodge, K., Bates, J., & Pettit, G. (1996). Physical discipline among African American and European American mothers: Links to children's externalizing behaviors. *Developmental Psychology, 32*(6), 1065–1072.

Denby, R. W., & Alford, K. A. (1996). Understanding African American discipline styles: Suggestions for effective social work intervention. *Journal of Multicultural Social Work, 4*(3), 81–98.

Doyle, S. R., & McCarty, C. A. (2001). *Child Behavior Checklist (Grade 7, Year 8 Update)* (Technical Report) [On-line]. Available: http://www.fasttrackproject .org/

Durrett, M. E., O'Bryant, S., & Pennebaker, J. (1975). Child-rearing reports of White, Black and Mexican American families. *Developmental Psychology, 11*, 871.

Gershoff, E. T., & Grogan-Kaylor, A. (2016b). Race as a moderator of associations between spanking and child outcomes. *Family Relations, 65*, 490–501.

Gershoff, E. T., Lansford, J. E., Sexton, H. R., Davis-Kean, P., & Sameroff, A. J. (2012). Longitudinal links between spanking and children's externalizing behaviors in a national sample of White, Black, Hispanic, and Asian American families. *Child Development, 83*, 838–843.

Greene, K., & Garner, P. (2012). African American mothers' disciplinary responses: Associations with family background characteristics, maternal childrearing attitudes, and child manageability. *Journal of Family Economic Issues, 33*, 400–409.

Hardy, K. V., & Laszloffy, T. A. (2005). *Teens Who Hurt: Clinical Interventions to Break the Cycle of Adolescent Violence*. New York: The Guilford Press.

Hill Collins, P. (2000). *Black Feminist Thought: Knowledge, Consciousness, and the Politics of Empowerment/Patricia Hill Collins*. (2nd ed., Rev. Tenth Anniversary ed.). New York, NY: Routledge.

Horn, I. B., Cheng, T. L., & Joseph, J. (2004). Discipline in the African American community: The impact of socioeconomic status on beliefs and practices. *Pediatrics, 113*, 1236–1241.

Ispa, J. M., & Halgunseth, L. C. (2004). Talking about corporal punishment: Nine low-income African American mothers' perspectives. *Early Childhood Research Quarterly, 19*, 463–484.

Joe, J. R., Shillingford-Butler, M. A., & Oh, S. (2019). The experiences of African American mothers raising sons in the context of #Black live matter. *The Professional Counselor, 9*(1), 67–79.

Johnson, R. L., & Stanford, P. (2002*). Strength for their Journey: Five Essential Disciplines African American Parents Must Teach Their Children and Teens*. Harlem Moon: New York.

Lansford, J. E., Deater-Deckard, K., Dodge, K. A., Bates, J. E., & Pettit, G. S. (2004). Ethnic differences in the link between physical discipline and later adolescent externalizing behaviors. *Journal of Child Psychology and Psychiatry, 45*, 801–812.

LeCuyer, E. A., Christensen, J. J., Kearney, M. H., & Kitzman, H. J. (2011). African American mothers' self-described discipline strategies with young children. *Issues in Comprehensive Pediatric Nursing, 34*, 144–162.

Kamii, C., & Radin, N. (1967). The child-rearing attitudes of disadvantaged Negro mothers and some educational implications. *Journal of Negro Education, 16,* 139–146.

McLoyd, V. C., Hardaway, C. R., & Jocson, R. M. (2019). African American Parenting. In *Handbook of Parenting*, Volume 4: Social Conditions and Applied Parenting Routledge Accessed on: 26 Aug 2019 https://www.routledgehandbooks .com/doi/10.4324/9780429398995-3

McLoyd, V. C., & Smith, J. (2002). Physical discipline and behavior problems in African American, European American, and Hispanic Children: Emotional support as a moderator. *Journal of Marriage and Family, 64*(1), 40–53.

Portes, P. R., Dunham, R. M., & Williams, S. (1986). Assessing child-rearing style in ecological settings: Its relation to culture, social class, early age intervention and scholastic achievement. *Adolescence, 21,* 723–735.

Radin, N., & Kamii, C. (1965). The childrearing attitudes of disadvantaged Negro mothers and some educational implications. *Journal of Negro Education, 34,* 138–146.

Richman, S. B., & Mandara, J. (2013). Do socialization goals explain differences in parental control between Black and White parents? *Family Relations, 62*(4), 625–636.

Roberts, D. (1997). *Killing the Black Body: Race, Reproduction, and the Meaning of Liberty.* New York, NY: Random House.

Roberts, D. (2002). *Shattered Bonds: The Color of Child Welfare/Dorothy Roberts.* New York, NY: Basic Books.

Roberts, D. (2011) Child protection as surveillance of African American families. *Journal of Social Welfare and Family Law, 36*(4), 426–437.

Roche, K. M., Ghazarian, S. R., Little, T. D., & Leventhal, T. (2010). Understanding links between punitive parenting and adolescent adjustment: The relevance of context and reciprocal associations. *Journal of Research on Adolescence, 21*(2), 448–460.

Skinner, O. D., & McHale, S. H. (2016). Parent-adolescent conflict in African American families. *Journal Youth Adolescence, 45,* 2080–2093.

Smetana, J., & Chuang, S. (2001). Middle-class African American parents' conceptions of parenting in early adolescence. *Journal of Research on Adolescence, 11*(2), 177–198.

Smetana, J., & Gaines, C. (1991). Adolescent-parent conflict in middle-class African American families. *Child Development, 70*(6), 1447–1463.

Stevenson, H. C., & Arrington, E. G. (2009). Racial/ethnic socialization mediates perceived racism and identity experiences of African American students. *Cultural Diversity and Ethnic Mental Health, 15,* 125–136.

Stevenson, H. C., Davis, G., & Abdul-Kabir, S. (2001). *Stickin" to, Watchn" Over, and Getting' With: An African American Parent's Guide to Discipline.* San Francisco: Josey Bass.

Streit, C., Custavo, C., Ispa, J. M., & Palermo, F. (2017). Negative emotionality and discipline as long-term predictors of behavioral outcomes in African American and European American children. *Developmental Psychology, 53*(6), 1013–1026.

Taylor, C., Hamvas, L., & Paris, R. (2011). Perceived instrumentality and normative-ness of corporal punishment use among Black mothers. *Family Relations, 60*(1), 60–72.

Thomas, K. A., & Dettlaff, A. J. (2011). African American families and the role of physical witnessing in the past in the present. *Journal of Human Behavior in the Social Environment, 21*, 963–977.

Chapter 3

Disciplinary Practices of African American Fathers

How we think of African American men as fathers is how we respond to them. African American fathers are considered to be the most misunderstood members of African American families (Coles & Green, 2010; Doyle et al., 2015; Hannon et al., 2015, 2017; Hines & Boyd-Franklin, 2005; Johnson, 2006, 2016; McAdoo, 1979, 1988). The scholarly and popular discourses have consistently depicted African American fathers as unwilling to provide or to take responsibility for their children, uninvolved in the lives of their children, and potentially violent (Hamer, 2001; Johnson, 2009, 2016; Gadsden et al., 2003; Wallace, 2017). Research has primarily focused on the "absence" instead of the "presence" of African American fathers, and African American men are rarely the source of data about their own parenthood experiences (Gadsden et al., 2003; Wallace, 2017). In fact, noted African American scholars have discussed the difficulty in publishing comments, observations, and findings regarding the active involvement of African American men in the lives of their children (e.g., Conner & White, 2006).

It is also important to underscore the less-than-equitable treatment that African American fathers face when dealing with human services and the legal system. Child welfare workers have been found to favor African American mothers over African American fathers when it comes to custody decisions, and tend to view African American men through a punitive lens when evaluating their past and present parenting behavior (Doyle et al., 2013, 2016; Grief, 2011). Further, O'Donnell et al. (2005) assert that African American fathers are often an afterthought when courts and child welfare workers deliberate over parenting concerns involving African American families.

Several historical and present-day investigations have offered correctives to the negative portrayal of African American fathers and their lack of inclusion in the overall evaluation of African American child-rearing practices. For example, the seminal work of McAdoo (1979, 1988) explored the role of African American fathers in the development and socialization of African American preschool-age children. While focusing on working- and middle-class families, McAdoo (1979) recorded in detail thirty-six father–child interactions in two home interviews. The findings revealed that a large majority of the participants' verbal interactions with their children were nurturant. Although the fathers in this study perceived themselves to be strict (expected their children to obey them right away, and had no tolerance for angry shouting or kicking from their children), their actual interaction patterns tended to be firm, warm, and nonpunitive. They also encouraged verbal interchange between themselves and their child, to the extent that fathers would sometimes interrupt the interviewer to answer the child's questions. African American fathers also shared equally with their wives in making decisions regarding their children. The children of the participants felt good about themselves, and felt that their fathers, mothers, and peers valued them highly.

Hamer and Marchioro (2002) examined African American fathers who have assumed primary care of their children, often referred to as custodial fathers. The research team interviewed twenty-four working-class, low-income, never-married, single-parenting African American men. Most of the fathers in their sample were the primary caretakers of only one child, but four had two children and one had three children. Often, the fathers obtained primary responsibility if the child was removed from the mother's household because of abuse or neglect, or if the children sought to live with their father. Fathers had to perform caregiving activities and discipline while also attending to the circumstance(s) that had led to obtaining custodial parenthood. Fathers were firm in establishing house rules and responsibilities for their children, but sometimes doubted whether they were making the right decisions or being too strict, especially with their adolescent daughters. When fathers felt that they had not correctly handled a parenting situation with their child, they often used social networks to check their own child-rearing practices and to reinforce their parenting strategies.

FATHERS WHO LIVE AWAY FROM THEIR CHILDREN

Some studies focused on the parenting practices of non-custodial fathers. For instance, Hamer (1997) examined the role of fatherhood among thirty-eight African American non-custodial fathers, and found that fathers provided emotional support and discipline for their children. Emotional support was demonstrated by fathers encouraging their children to do well in school, expressing enthusiasm for their child's accomplishments, and attending school functions as often as possible. The fathers in this study expected respect and honesty from their children. Discipline was often conducted by talking with their children about "right and wrong" behaviors. In 2001, Hamer interviewed eighty-eight African American fathers whom she referred to as Black live-away fathers. She provides below a contextual lens into the caregiving activities of these fathers:

> According to the fathers in this study, "ideal" live-away fathers are those who spend as much time as possible with their children. This they perceived, was their primary paternal function . . . Most of these fathers attempted to involve themselves as much as possible in the daily aspects of their children's care . . . They picked their children up after school, counseled them, and listened to their concerns. They prepared their meals and helped with homework. When they felt mothers were weak in terms of disciplining their children, they stepped in to fill the void. (Hamer, 2001)

However, Hamer also acknowledged that the fathers in her study often had to negotiate their parenting activities in the midst of "unfriendly attitudes and behaviors" from the mothers of their children, as well as varied employment schedules. More recent studies (Hammond et al., 2011; Julion et al., 2012) of non-resident fathers highlighted the father's role as a nurturer through moral guidance and the teaching of critical life lessons.

However, even with the emerging research on the active parenting of African American fathers, much of the public discourse still views African American fathers as absent from the lives of their children. In 2015, a *New York Times* article written by journalist and commentator Charles Blow shed light on the inaccuracy of this popular misconception. Specifically, Blow (2015) highlighted recent data from the Centers for Disease Control and Prevention (CDC) showing that the majority of African American births were to unmarried mothers. He was quick to point out, however, that mothers not being married to the child's father does not necessarily equate to a lack of father involvement in African American homes.

Blow illustrates his point by highlighting the results of the 2013 National Health Statistics Report (Jones et al., 2013), co-published by the U.S. Department of Health and Human Services (DHHS) and the Centers for Disease Control and Prevention (CDC), on father involvement. In this study of fathers living with children and fathers living away from their children, Black fathers more often than White and Hispanic Fathers fed or ate meals with their children daily, played with their children daily, and transported their children to or from various activities. In fact, Perry et al. (2012), in their study of African American fathers in co-resident family formations, found that unwed cohabiting fathers were more involved with their children than married fathers. The strongest predictor of married fathers' involvement was paternal self-assessment, which is to say that fathers who perceived themselves more positively predicted higher levels of involvement. For unwed co-habiting fathers, receiving higher levels of support from their child's mother significantly predicted a high level of involvement from the father.

Some scholars have argued that the conventional meaning of fatherhood underestimates the role of African American fathers. According to Caldwell and White (2006), the traditional perspective of being a father does not adequately capture the cultural nuances that surround the fathering role in the African American community. They suggested the use of the term "social fathering" to more appropriately depict the parenting activities of African American men. Social fathering encompasses biological fathers as the most important group, but also includes men who are not biological fathers (e.g., grandfathers, brother, uncle, godfathers, half-brothers, cousins, and ministers). These men assume all of the roles that fathers are expected to perform (Conner & White, 2006, 2012).

McDougal and George (2016) explored the parenting experiences of twenty-four Black social fathers. In explaining the most significant influences that the participants had over their non-biological children's lives, they identified love and care, as well as the value of education and discipline. Some social fathers acknowledged major disagreements with biological fathers over conflicting disciplinary styles, rules, and values, which sometimes led to authority disputes between the biological and social fathers. Social fathers also reported that, because they were not their children's biological fathers, their position was often questioned by the children or undermined by the biological father's or the mother's extended family members.

A CLOSER LOOK AT CHILD DISCIPLINE

One of the greatest influences that many African American fathers have on their children is instilling within them a sense of discipline (McDougal & George, 2016). African American fathers have a distinct way of disciplining children, but investigations exclusively examining the disciplinary practices of African American fathers have been few. My previous research has shown that African American fathers, use "discuss matters with their children" as a primary disciplinary technique (Bradley, 2000; Adkison-Johnson et al., 2016). Other techniques, such as "give warning look," "order child not to," "withdraw privileges," and "give extra work," are also used, depending on the age of the child and the child's transgression. Specifically, fathers designated "discuss matter with child," "order child not to," and "give warning look" as the preferred disciplinary methods with their preschool-age children (three to five). As the child becomes older, fathers increase their use of discussions and the withdrawal of privileges with their elementary-age children, and employ withdrawal of privileges substantially more with their adolescents.

It is important to note that my previous research has shown that African American fathers use physical discipline considerably less than African American mothers. When physical discipline is used, African American fathers exclusively spank their preschool-age children, mainly boys, with an open hand. Techniques such as "spank with switch," "whip with belt," "slap child in face," and "ignore child" were among the disciplinary methods least likely to be used by African American fathers. It is also worth noting that there are distinct differences between African American fathers and mothers when it comes to child discipline. In my 2016 investigation of the disciplinary practices of 189 African American mothers and fathers, I examined the differences between African American fathers' and mothers' responses in relation to child misbehavior. Specifically, I wanted to understand differences in parent response to repeated misbehavior. By utilizing the African American Child Discipline Survey (which I created), each parent responded to twelve hypothetical parenting situations that varied by the age of the child (preschool, elementary, adolescent, and late adolescent) and the severity of the disciplinary transgression (mild, moderate, and severe). Participants were asked to select from a list of disciplinary strategies (e.g., "discuss matter with child," "demand/order child not to do it again," "warn child they will receive a spanking/whuppin," "withdrawal privileges," "spank with open hand," or "whup child with a belt or switch") that they would use to resolve each of the contextual situations, as well as what their second response would be if the child (in the hypothetical parenting situation) repeated the misbehavior.

Overall, the study found that African American fathers used less severe disciplinary methods than African American mothers across all contextual situations. Specifically, fathers used "discuss" (e.g., discuss matter with child) as a first and second response in addressing the same contextual situation with preschool-age children, whereas mothers primarily used techniques such as "demand child not to do it again" as a first response and spanking as a second response to address moderate contextual situations (e.g., running out in front of a car) for their preschool-age (three to five) children. Fathers also differed in their approach in addressing adolescent (twelve to fourteen) repeated misbehavior, and used significantly less concrete disciplinary methods than mothers. In detail, for severe adolescent disciplinary situations (e.g., child called parent a nasty name after being told they couldn't go to a concert), fathers used "discuss and warn" as their first and second disciplinary actions, with mothers using spanking as a first and second response to address this particular misbehavior. Several studies have affirmed that African American fathers are effective in utilizing a "discussion approach" because of their insistence on respect from their children, and that their children understood (from an early age) that inappropriate behavior would not be tolerated (Coles & Green, 2010; Daddis & Smetana, 2005; Hamer, 1997).

As mentioned in chapter 1, my most recent investigation spotlights what African American parents are currently doing regarding child discipline and behavioral expectations. The eleven African American fathers involved in this investigation were fathers of preschool-age (three to five), elementary (six to eleven), preadolescent (twelve to fourteen), and late-adolescent (fifteen to seventeen) children. Participants comprised both one-parent and two-parent households. Family size ranged from one to four children, and children's ages ranged from two to seventeen. Most of the fathers had completed between some college and a college degree. The average household income level was $40,000–$59,999, with the majority of fathers from household incomes of $60,000 and up. Given the risk involved in discussing actual disciplinary practices and/or responses, names and titles have been replaced by pseudonyms. Quotes are presented in the vernacular in which they were spoken. Two themes were identified from the interviews: *Authority: There is only one man in this house* and *Adjusting child behavior.*

AUTHORITY: THERE IS ONLY ONE MAN IN THIS HOUSE

The notion of authority for these fathers meant that they were responsible for preparing their children to be leaders of their own destinies. Prominent African American psychologist Dr. Na'im Akbar (2017) stressed the importance of African American parents, especially fathers, unequivocally taking responsibility for their children:

> The old folks (our foreparents) took charge of their children's lives. They didn't let them stay up all night . . . You must take responsibility of parenthood seriously by taking charge of your children decisively. Your child says, "Daddy, I don't like spinach." Tell him, "Eat it anyway!" When he asks why, tell him, "It's good for you and, most importantly, I said so!" He will eat it. He may not love it and one day he may choose not to eat it, but as long as he's operating in your house (kingdom), he must do as the king and queen say. When he is no longer in the kingdom, he can go into the desert and find his own kingdom. But as long as he is there, he must obey the authority in the house. (p. 60)

Fathers in this study depicted authority as providing safety and building character and discernment so that their children can fulfill their purpose in life. This was evident for social fathers as well as biological fathers. Children receiving prescribed behavior expectations facilitated this process. Henry, the father of elementary-age and adolescent children, states that, "For me, you define what the expectations are for them. When they are outside, consistently, of expectations, they cross the line." Problematic behaviors such as lying, stealing, talking back, negative tone of voice, having an attitude, and being defiant were identified as "cross the line" behaviors. For example, Henry described the way he addressed lying and stealing with his ten-year-old: "I told him . . . I can't trust anybody that would lie to me or steal from me . . . this is what lying and stealing, ultimately, can lead to; someone else, probably, is gonna lock you up or kill you."

African American poet, educator, and publisher Haki Madhubuti (1991) shared his behavior expectations for his children. And although these rules were published almost three decades ago, these standards were explicit in the parenting practices of many fathers in this study:

1. *Don't lie, don't steal, don't cheat.*
2. *Don't embarrass your family; listen to your parents and other responsible adults.*
3. *Always do your best and improve on yesterday's work; develop a work attitude.*
4. *Learn as much as you can; always expand your knowledge base.*
5. *Seek quality in all things rather than weakening quantity.*
6. *Always be creative; do not settle for easy answers or conclusions. Think for yourself and learn to be responsible for your decisions.*
7. *Learn from mistakes and always oppose that which is not good.*
8. *Do homework and housework each day.*
9. *Avoid alcohol, drugs, and cigarettes.*
10. *Respect elders.*
11. *Be a self-starter, self-motivator; do not wait on others to set high goals/standards for you. Always seek the best and avoid the "crowd" mentality.*
12. *Never forget who you are and always speak up if you feel that you have been wronged.* (pp. 195–196)

ADJUSTING CHILD BEHAVIOR

Fathers invested a significant amount time adjusting the deposition and disobedient conduct of their children. Table 3.1 is a list of problematic behaviors

Table 3.1 Problematic Behaviors versus What Fathers Do

Problematic Behaviors	What Fathers Do
Mumbling under their breath after father told them to do something (son, age twelve)	"First, make sure I heard correctly, reminded him you don't pay no bills . . . if you do it again . . . you probably need to figure out how to pay your own bills."
Talking back (daughter, age ten)	"I reminded her that (I am the father) she is a child. I start taking the TV off the wall, took the phone, everything."
Telling them to do something and they pout (son, age four, and daughter, age six)	"Okay, why are you crying? Do we need to give you something to cry about? Because right now you're just crying."
Telling child to do something and they have an attitude (facial expression) (son, age eleven, and daughter, age thirteen)	"Is something wrong with your face? Now I want to go to your room, but not hearing nothing being thrown or dropped or door closing hard."
Child directly challenges father's authority (son, age sixteen)	"I took it to him . . . He never did it again."
Daughter preoccupied with boys (daughter, age fifteen)	"You gotta focus . . . focus on your (school) work. Leave those boys alone."

Created by Author.

and the actual disciplinary strategies that the fathers used in order to address the child's conduct.

The fathers in this study paid particular attention to their child's communication. Ronald shares his experience changing how his teenager communicated with other people:

> Well, the other day, my son, he doesn't like to talk. He's a real bad introvert. He hates talking. So I'm trying to bring him out of that. I make him talk. But the other day, he had some type of attitude for whatever reason. Just being a teen or whatever. His mother was speaking to him, but he tries to cut her off and answer questions before they're even asked and stuff like that. I told him, "You don't have no more time today. You let somebody talk to you, you assess it, and then you answer. You don't just blurt out answers just because you don't want to talk." It's more of an attitude with him like that . . . I've been seeing him trying to do it again and then he remembers . . . *I told him* you always have the think, and you always have to be aware of what you're doing.

The men in this study also "checked" their sons' "mumbling under their breath," even if it meant correcting the child in front of their friends. Derrick shares the following example:

I said . . . make sure your room is clean. Something—I heard him say something. So, I was like, "Did you say something?" And he got quiet. So, I said it again. By this time, I'm—I know he just—not just say this. So, I'm walking back. By the time I got to where he was at, he's like, "No, I was just—" And I was like, "I didn't ask you question. So, I don't think you need to respond." And then later his friends was joking to him about the situation.

It is important to note that fathers living with or away from their children reported that their child's mother was more permissive in their parenting. This finding is consistent with a study by Doyle et al. (2014) regarding the co-parenting experiences of African American fathers, which found that fathers were concerned about the mothers giving in to their sons' requests and not holding them accountable for their actions. However, there were some fathers in this current study who also raised this parenting style difference in relation to their daughters. Cornell, the father of a preschool-age daughter, explains, "Whatever I ask her is not a problem; she does it. She's not wild; she's not running around, loud . . . but when she at her mother's house . . . she's screaming at the top her lungs . . . running the house . . . And so to me, I want to curb that. You're still supposed to do what you're supposed to do—no running in the house, no hollering in the house."

Some fathers noted that mothers viewed the fathers as being too hard on their daughters regarding disciplinary responses. Leonard explains:

My oldest daughter was acting up in school. She is an angel around me . . . my wife didn't understand why I was so upset. I don't know what you would call it, clever, slick behavior . . . Because she know she been at the school acting buck wild. I told her . . . You got me thinking everything is fine at school. And all the time you know I only reward good behavior and you know you've been showing your ass. I don't care if the computer broke . . . You will not get another one . . . my wife thought I overreacted.

NARRATIVE IN DETAIL

In order to provide a comprehensive picture of the ways in which African American fathers approach child discipline, I will describe one narrative in greater detail. Daryl is a compilation of the disciplinary experiences shared by the various fathers who participated in the study. This case study describes the mundane as well as the complex ways that African American fathers navigate their parenting styles in order to shape the behaviors of their children.

Daryl is a thirty-seven-year-old father of a sixteen-year-old son and a fifteen-year-old daughter, and shares custody with the children's mother.

Daryl was married to his children's mother for three years, although they lived together for four years prior to the marriage. Daryl maintains steady work and recently purchased his first home. He graduated from high school and completed one year of community college. Daryl had a pretty good childhood with both parents, until his mom died when he was thirteen. His mother had a long battle with cancer, so his aunts and uncles stepped in to assist his dad with child-rearing responsibilities. Daryl's father worked hard to financially support his family, and he expected all of his children to live up to their potential. Daryl's father, as well as his aunts and uncles, were "no nonsense" disciplinarians. Children were expected to complete assigned chores, and to be respectful toward each other and adults. Daryl could only remember one whuppin from his father, after Daryl and his friends were found playing with matches in the basement that started a small fire. Most of his punishments were "being grounded" and "having to do additional chores." When the interviewer asked Daryl about child discipline practices and the parenting goals for his children, he answered,

When my children were small, discipline was pretty easy. I told my children when they stay with me I have my own rules. Their mother's parenting is okay, but I started early on making sure they knew what was expected of them. When my daughter was four, she had to complete her food before leaving the table. I didn't have all day to wait for her to finish so she had a set time before she knew she might get in trouble. I would threaten her with a spanking although I never really spanked her. My son was fine when he was little, but I had some behavior problems with him several months ago. He stopped completing his homework and he was hanging out with a group of friends that are not focused.

Last month he had an attitude and was yelling at his sister. I had to stop him from spending time at a friends' house because he started saying "what" when I called his name, instead of saying "yes" or "yes dad" like he used to. It all came to a head three weeks ago when I heard him yelling at his sister because she asked to use his laptop to complete her homework assignment. I went into his room and said, "Didn't I tell you not to yell at her?" And so I said, "Give me your video games, give me your laptop and the phone. You're grounded!" He went to huffing and puffing, got closer to me, looked me up and down like he wanted to do something. Right then, I grabbed him by the shirt and pushed him up against the wall and got directly in his face and said, "This is my house. I am your father. Don't you ever in your life try that again!" I put him out of my house and called his mother to come get him. She refused, after she heard what happened, but called a neighbor who is a good friend of hers so he would not get picked up by the police. I called my father to calm down, and he told me to not let him back into the house until my son understood his place in this family. My son called me the next day and apologized for his behavior. I accepted his apology, because I know he knew better. However, I told him there would still be consequences for his actions. He is now grounded for the next three months at my house and his mothers. No privileges except to go to school, few meals each day, and think about what he is going to do with his life. Since that incident, I continue to talk to him like I always have done about the importance of using good judgement . . . you are made in the image of God . . . a leader . . . not a follower. My son has the potential to do great things with his life. He is a good kid, but was starting to go down the wrong path. I had to get him straight.

Daryl asked the interviewer if she knew someone that could help him figure out "what's going on" with his son.

A dearth of information is available regarding how best to address late-adolescent problematic behavior. Daryl's monitoring and child-rearing activities were consistent with previous studies that reported that African American fathers play an active role in establishing behavior standards for the preschool-age, elementary-age, and adolescent children. Involvement includes correction and holding teenagers accountable for their actions without breaking their spirit (Stevenson et al., 2001). Stevenson et al. (2001) recommend that parents apply accountability instead of punishment. They define *accountability* as a "refined type of discipline that reflects consistent closeness and caring, along with a sense of commitment, acceptance of responsibility, a balanced doling out of consequences, and an honoring of the community and Creator as the highest authority" (p. 12). Table 3.2 illustrates Stevenson and colleagues' punishment versus accountability.

This perspective accounts for the centrality of spirituality and community in the African American worldview (Akbar, 2017). In fact, Cook (1996), in his writings about spiritually minded fathers, illustrates this point in terms of fathers providing spiritual direction:

Table 3.2 Punishment versus Accountability

Punishment	Accountability
1. Retribution is the focus.	1. Restoration is the focus.
2. Suffering is greater than learning.	2. Learning is greater than suffering.
3. Relationship is unnecessary.	3. Relationship is essential.
4. Consequences are managed alone.	4. Consequences are managed within the community.
5. Society is the higher authority.	5. Community and Creator are the higher authority.

Created by Author.

When we talk, as spiritually minded parents, of the path we have traveled and are traveling, it is not to demand that our children take a similar path or that they take a path we might or should have taken. It is to extract the lessons of spiritual growth and development we have learned and are learning along our way. It is to illuminate how experiences can give rise to greater intimacy with an acknowledgment of the infinite that transcends yet pervades our infinite experience. We understand that every path has its own unique experiences. Those experiences, whether pleasant or unpleasant, have a place in our spiritual evolution when we see with spiritual eyes, listen with spiritual ears, and attune our souls to the call of the Devine. Thus, children who have spiritual guides as parents follow their parents, not out of fear or custom but because, like moths in darkness they are drawn to the light. They find in their parents' experiences and wisdom something their souls once knew but forgot, or something they should know but do not, or something the will know but do not yet. In this spiritual understanding of parenting, parents are liberated from the fear of losing control of their children, for they were never theirs to control from the start. Children are liberated from the fears of conditional love, those demons that destroy both body and soul. In this space void of fear, a true love takes hold that no poet or psalmist could treat justly. It is a love that passes all understanding and covers the multitude of faults, foibles, and failures to which the imperfect art of parenting gives rise. (pp. 25–26)

Although respect for authority is a cultural value within many African American families, it becomes a challenge when adolescents are only a few years from adulthood. Adolescence is a dangerous time for young African American men. The general bias, dismissive treatment from classroom teachers, and the overall presumption by the police that young African American men are inherently criminal complicates this particular stage of development. Teenagers undergo many psychological, biological (physical changes), and social challenges that could cause periods of frustration, and sometimes rage, when life circumstances are presented in such a way that seems unfair (Hardy & Laszloffy, 2007; Poussaint & Comer, 1992). According to Hardy and Laszloffy, adolescents exhibiting acting-out or rebellious behaviors are lightning rods for most of the adults regularly interacting with them. These behaviors are often worrisome, because they flirt with crossing the lines of moral decency. The work of Dr. Kenneth V. Hardy (e.g., *Teens Who Hurt: Clinical Interventions to Break The Cycle Of Adolescent Violence*) is a great resource for restoring and strengthening parent–adolescent relationships. Although it is important that parents seek to understand the causes of their child's frustration, they must also send a clear message that teenagers communicate their frustrations in a respectful manner.

The Daryl narrative shows us that context matters in the way he disciplined his son, and that a "quick rush to judgment" only hinders one's understanding of the parenting situation. This also challenges the misconception of African American fathers that sees them as violent or harsh disciplinarians.

REFERENCES

Adkison-Bradley, C. (2011). Seeing African Americans as competent parents: Implications for marriage and family counselors. *The Family Journal, 19*, 307–313.

Adkison-Bradley, C., Terpstra, J., & Dormitorio, B. (2014). Child discipline in African American families: A study of patterns and context. *The Family Journal, 22*, 198–205.

Adkison-Johnson, C. (2019). *Exploring Child Discipline: Effectiveness of a Counseling Group for African American Parents.* Chicago, IL: American Psychological Association Annual Convention.

Adkison-Johnson, C., Terpstra, J., Burgos, J., & Payne, D. (2016). African American child discipline: Differences between mothers and fathers. *Family Court Review, 54*(2), 203–220.

Akbar, N. (2017). *New Visions for Black Men.* Tallahassee, FL: Mind Productions.

Anderson, J. E. (1936). *The Young Child in the Home.* White House Conference on Child Health and Protection, Committee on the Infant and Pre-school Child. New York: Appleton-Century.

Baker, C. R. (2017). Father-son relationships in ethnically diverse families: Links to boys' cognitive and social emotional development in preschool. *Journal of Child and Family Studies, 26*(8), 2335–2345.

Bartz, K. W., & Levine, E. S. (1978). Child rearing by Black parents: A description and comparison to Anglo and Chicano parents. *Journal of Marriage and the Family, 40*, 709–719.

Belgrave, F. Z., & Allison, K. W. (2019). *African American Psychology: From Africa to. America.* Los Angeles, CA: Sage.

Bluestone, C., & Tamis-Lemonda, C. (1999). Correlates of parenting styles in predominantly working- and middle-class African American mothers. *Journal of Marriage and Family, 61*(4), 881–893.

Blow, C. M. (2015, June 8). Black dads are doing best of all. *The New York Times.* https://www.nytimes.com/

Boyd-Franklin, N. (2003). *Black Families in Therapy: Understanding the African American Experience.* New York, NY: Guilford Press.

Boyd-Franklin, N., & Bry, B. H. (2000). *Reaching Out in Family Therapy: Home-Based, School, and Community Interventions.* New York: The Guilford Press.

Bradley, C. R. (1998). Child rearing in African American families: A study of disciplinary methods used by African American parents. *Journal of Multicultural Counseling and Development, 26*, 273–281.

Bradley, C. R. (2000). The disciplinary practices of African American fathers: A closer look. *Journal of African American Men, 5*, 43–61.

Caldwell, L. D., & White, J. L. (2006). Generative fathering: Challenges to Black Masculinity and identity. In M. Conner & L. Joseph (Eds.), *Black Fathers: An Invisible Presence in America* (pp. 53–69). Mahwah, NJ: Lawrence Erlbaum Associates Publishers.

Coles, R. L., & Green, C. (2010). *The Myth of the Missing Black Father*. New York: Columbia University Press.

Cook, A. E. (1996). From boys to men: Breaking the cycle of pain for our sons. In A. Willis (Eds.), *Faith of Our Fathers: African American Men Reflect on Fatherhood* (pp. 21–42). New York: Dutton Books.

Connor, M., & White, J. (2006). *Black Fathers: An Invisible Presence in America*. Mahwah, NJ: Lawrence Erlbaum Associates.

Connor, M. E., & White, J. L. (2012). *Black Fathers: An Invisible Presence in America* (2nd Ed.). New York, NY: Routledge.

Doyle, O., Clark, T., Cryer-Coupet, Q., Nebbitt, V., Goldston, D., Estroff, S., & Magan, I. (2015). Unheard Voices: African American Fathers Speak About Their Parenting Practices. *Psychology of Men & Masculinity, 16*(3), 274–283.

Doyle, O., Estroff, S., Goldston, D., Dzirasa, E., Fontes, M., & Burriss, A. (2013). "You gotta have a good help mate": African American fathers' co-parenting experiences. *Psychology of Men & Masculinity, 15*(4), 377–386.

Doyle, O., Magan, I., Cryer-Coupet, Q., Goldston, D., & Estroff, S. (2016). "Don't wait for it to rain to buy an umbrella": The transmission of values from African American fathers to sons. *Psychology of Men & Masculinity, 17*(4), 309.

Gadsden, V., Wortham, S., & Turner, H. (2003). Situated identities of young, African American fathers in low-income urban settings. *Family Court Review, 41*(3), 381–399.

Greif, G., Jones, J., Worthy, J., White, E., Davis, W., & Pitchford, E. (2011). Working with urban, African American fathers: The importance of service provision, joining, accountability, the father-child relationship, and couples work. *Journal of Family Social Work, 14*(3), 247–261.

Gray, S. S., & Nybell, L. M. (1990). Issues in African American family preservation. *Child Welfare, 56*, 513–523.

Hamer, J. F. (1997). The fathers of "fatherless" Black children. *Families in Society, 78*(6), 564–578.

Hamer, J. F. (2001). *What It Means to be Daddy: Fatherhood for Black Men Living Away From Their Children*. New, NY: Columbia University Press.

Hamer, J. F., & Marchoro, K. (2002). Becoming custodial dads: Exploring parenting among low-income and working-class African American fathers. *Journal of Marriage and Family, 64*, 116–129.

Hammond, W., Caldwell, C., Brooks, C., & Bell, L. (2011). Being there in spirit, fire, and mind: Expressive roles among nonresidential African American fathers. *Research on Social Work Practice, 21*(3), 308–318.

Hannon, M. D., Blanchard, R., & Storlie, C. (Spring 2019). Microaggression experiences of fathers with children with autism spectrum disorder. *The Family Journal: Counseling and Therapy for Couples and Families, 27*(2), 199–208. doi: 10.1177/1066480719832512

Hannon, M. D., White, E., & Nadrich, T. (Spring 2017a). Influences of autism on fathering style among Black American fathers: A narrative inquiry. *Journal of Family Therapy, 39*(2), 1–23. doi: 10.1111/1467-6427.12165

Hardy, K., & Laszloffy, T. (2005). *Teens Who Hurt: Clinical Interventions to Break the Cycle of Adolescent Violence*. New York: Guilford Press.

Hines, P. M., & Boyd-Franklin, N. (2005) African American families. In M. McGoldrick, Giordano, J., & Garcia-Preto, N. (Eds.), *Ethnicity and Family Therapy* (pp. 87–100). NY: The Guildford Press.

Hutchinson, E. O. (1995). *Black Fatherhood: The Guide to Male Parenting*. Los Angeles: Middle Passage Press.

Johnson, P. D. (2006). Counseling Black men: A contextualized humanistic approach. *Counseling and Values, 50*, 187–196. doi:10.1002/j.2161-007X.2006.tb00055.x

Johnson, P. D. (2016). Somebodiness and Its Meaning to African American Men. *Journal of Counseling and Development, 94*, 333–344.

Jones, J., Mosher, W., & National Center for Health Statistics, issuing body. (2013). *Fathers' Involvement with Their Children: United States, 2006–2010 /* by Jo Jones, and William D. Mosher. (National health statistics reports ; no. 71). U.S. Department of Health and Human Services, Centers for Disease Control and Prevention, National Center for Health Statistics.

Julion, W. A., Breitenstein, S. M., & Waddell, D. (2012), Fatherhood intervention development in collaboration with African American non-resident fathers. *Research. Nursing and Health, 35*, 490–506. doi: 10.1002/nur.21492

Madhubuti, H. (1990). *Black Men: Obsolete, Single, Dangerous?* Chicago: Third World Press.

McAdoo, J. (1979). A study of father-child interaction patterns and self-esteem in Black pre-school children. *Young Children, 34*(1), 46–53.

McAdoo, J. (1988). The roles of Black fathers in the socialization of Black children. In H. P. McAdoo (Ed.), *Black Families* (pp. 183–197). Newbury Park, CA: Sage Publications.

Mcdougal, S., & George, C. (2016). "I wanted to return the favor": The experiences and perspectives of Black social fathers. *Journal of Black Studies, 47*(6), 524–549.

O'Donnell, J. M., Johnson, W. E., D'Aunno, L. E., & Thornten, H. L. (2005). Fathers in child welfare: Caseworkers' perspectives. *Child Welfare, 84*(3), 387–414.

Perry, A., Harmon, D., & Leeper, J. (2012). Resident Black fathers' involvement: A comparative analysis of married and unwed, cohabitating fathers. *Journal of Family Issues, 33*(6), 695–714.

Ransaw, T. (2014). The good father: African American fathers who positively influence the educational outcomes of their children. *Spectrum: A Journal on Black Men, 2*(2), 1–25.

Stevenson, H. C., Davis, G., & Abdul-Kabir, S. (2001). *Stickin" to, Watchn" Over, and Getting' With: An African American Parent's Guide to Discipline*. San Francisco: Josey Bass.

Wallace, D. (2017). Distinctiveness, deference and dominance in Black Caribbean fathers' engagement with public schools in London and New York City. *Gender and Education, 29*(5), 594–613.

Chapter 4

Forging a United Front

Mothers and Fathers Working Together

Most of the writing and research on African American child discipline is focused on one-parent households. Either the mother or father lives alone with their children, or the father lives away from his children. This chapter will examine the context of child discipline in two-parent African American households. Few studies have provided insight into how African American mothers and fathers work together in order to fulfill their child discipline goals. Although the earlier work of Smetana (Smetana & Gaines, 1999; Smetana et al., 2005) and the more recent research of Mandara (Mandara et al., 2010, 2012) have provided valuable information on adolescent-parent conflict and gender differences in African American families, child disciplinary patterns and practices were not the essential focal point of the discussion.

Doyle et al. (2014) studied African American co-parenting from the perspective of residential and some non-residential fathers of at-risk pre-adolescent male youth. Many residential fathers in their study (fathers who lived with their sons) noted subtle differences between their son's mother and themselves regarding their approach to discipline. Fathers reported using stricter disciplinary approaches than their sons' mothers. One participant stated: "I am an old school type dude. I don't do a whole bunch of talking. I only talk once . . . And that's where we get in disagreements right there; cause she's more of the talk, time-out type" (p. 381). Some fathers who did not live with their son's mother voiced concern that their efforts to discipline their sons were undone when they would visit their mother, because of the permissiveness of the mother. One participant stated, "And it was driving me crazy cause when they come back to me, it always had to be discipline, discipline, discipline, cause they would get off" (p. 382). Overall, fathers acknowledged consistency between parents, shared rules, and common standards of parenting, despite the fathers' residence, marital status, or both. Jackson et al.

(2019) also found active involvement of non-resident fathers in co-parenting, and they also discovered that the father's sustained participation buffered the adverse consequences of stressful conditions on single mothers. Forhand et al. (2015) examined the firm control parenting of African American men who are co-habiting partners, finding that these social fathers collaborated with mothers both in setting and enforcing rules at home.

In focusing specifically on child discipline, my 2016 study found that child discipline differences were based on whether mothers and fathers lived in the same household. In other words, African American mothers who were not in the same household as the child's father were more purposeful in determining appropriate responses in addressing misbehavior. Specifically, African American mothers and fathers differed in their approach with preschool-age and adolescent children, in that African American fathers consistently used less restrictive methods (e.g., discuss matter with child) in order to address repeated misbehaviors. This finding is consistent with prior literature that indicated that African American fathers in general, and African American non-custodial and low-income fathers in particular, provide structure, nurturing, insight, and support in order to address problematic behaviors (Cole, 2009, 2010; Hamer, 1997; Hamer & Marchiro, 2002).

In comparison to African American mothers, African American fathers are least likely to use physical discipline for mild or even serious child infractions (Bradley, 2000; Daddis & Smetana, 2005; Peterson et al., 1998). Several studies have affirmed that African American fathers are effective in utilizing a "discussion approach" because of their insistence on respect from their children, and that their children understood (from an early age) that inappropriate behavior would not be tolerated (Coles, 2010; Daddis & Smetana, 2005; Hamer, 1997). This particular child-rearing difference among mothers and fathers seems to get activated or even exacerbated when African American parents are not living together, in light of the fact that gender differences were not related with two parents living in the same home. A plausible explanation for this outcome is that African American mothers and fathers who live in the same household may present a relatively "united front" in terms of addressing misbehavior (Daddis & Smetana, 2005). Mothers may be charged with the role of being the "first responder" in addressing problematic behaviors, while fathers, albeit aware of the child's disobedience and the mother's response, may assume the role as the last resort disciplinarian.

HOW COUPLES ADDRESS CHILD MISBEHAVIOR

In this book so far, I have presented a relevant portrayal of the disciplinary practices utilized by mothers and fathers. I would likewise like to share a portion of my discoveries related to how parents address the misbehavior of their children as a team, since the available writing on African American child discipline has fundamentally been centered around the perspectives of one parent. I had the opportunity to interview nine couples. The family size ranged from one to four children, and the children's ages ranged from two to seventeen. Most of the parents had completed between some college and an advanced college degree, and the average household income level was $60,000–$79,999. Given the risk involved in discussing actual disciplinary practices and/or responses and concerns about the couples being identified, names have been replaced by pseudonyms. Quotes are presented in the vernacular in which they were spoken. Two themes were identified from the interviews: *We work as a team* and *We are not on the same page*.

WE WORK AS A TEAM

A common theme conveyed by the participants was that they worked together to address the behaviors of their children. The participants demonstrated this by articulating distinct discipline roles in this collaborative process. John and Barbara stated the following:

John: It's formal and informal. As a general rule, she's gonna bring me up to speed either before or after the discipline situation. But she's gonna go in first more than likely. My approach has always been not to react, just see how it plays out first . . . how it naturally progresses.

Barbara: My approach has been to address the situation immediately. I let him know what happened in case he wants to add to the punishment.

John: She's the lawyer for the kids.

Barbara: Yes, I'm the prosecuting attorney.

However, some participants focused more on the contrast in disciplinary styles between the two parents, as illustrated by Donald and Sheri:

Donald: It's two different styles. They'll push her to the point where she responds. If I see an issue, I'm going to respond . . . I might give them some leeway, but I don't think we need to walk around the house saying, "Okay, you all need to pick that up. Pick that up. Pick that up." So it's to the point where we've asked over and over, and over and over, again. So now, I'm to the point where if I see it, I'm throwing it away. It doesn't matter what it is. Shoes, hats, coats . . . if it's out of order, the kids are like, "Where's my . . .." It's gone . . . It's gone. I deal with it directly.

Sheri: Because I might say, "Get that ball. Pick up that ball. Pick up that ball. Pick up that ball. Didn't I say pick up that ball?" That's what I get. He's like, "Okay, the ball going to be gone next time I see it." And I'm thinking, "Wait a minute, we paid for that ball." And he's like, "I don't care. The ball is gone."

The contrast in disciplinary styles is supported by previous research that found that African American mothers are the first responders in addressing child misbehavior in two-parent families. The responses from John and Donald underscore the swift and direct approach, as demonstrated by African American fathers in previous studies (e.g., Adkison-Johnson et al., 2016; Barnes, 1985; Doyle et al., 2013; Doyle, 2015; Peters, 1976).

UNITED FRONT WHEN PARENTS DISAGREE ON DISCIPLINARY APPROACH

Although there was an understanding among couples to support each other's parenting, there were times when the united front happened amid mothers and fathers contradicting how the other parent disciplined the child. Doris and Isiah explained the following:

Doris: The other week, I had to discipline my teenage daughter for cussing and being disrespectful. I told her my first thought was to slap her face. I told her my mother would have slapped me for cussing in her house. But I told my daughter we are not a violent household. You don't even see your Dad and I fight like that or use profanity. But understand . . . that's a button you pushed (me slapping you) when you decide you are going say what you say and any way you want to say it . . . I'm your mother . . . And I don't want you to keep acting like that. So as a result, you are grounded for the next month. My hope is that you think twice about what you did. You know . . . it made me feel very vulnerable just to say that to my daughter . . . you know . . . what I was thinking and feeling.

Isiah: Well, my approach on that was different. I actually disagreed with how she handled that and what she was saying, but I would never tell our daughter. Even if I, in my head, like, hmm, I don't think I would have told my daughter that . . . Because what I also know is that I know my wife's intentions in her heart. And if she's wrong, it's not gonna be a disaster. I'm gonna watch it. I'm not gonna let it just fall apart. But God was still bless it because we are trying to be a team . . . a family . . . But our kids won't ever know that I disagreed with this or if they do, it's gonna be so far down the road; like, yeah, we probably could have handled that a little bit different or whatever, but they won't know at that moment for sure . . . If one of us is wrong . . . we're wrong together. For a couple of reasons; one, the kids need to see us united. But the other reason is that the kids are not gonna be there forever.

The majority of the couples in this study wanted to send a clear message to their children that the parents were intimately working together to direct the family system, and that no children should interfere with that process. These parents discussed how they managed their differences with each other away from their children, because it was considered a "grown folk" conversation. Another dimension of the family relationship is vulnerability, as described by Hardy and Laszloffy (2005):

> Vulnerability paves the pathways to emotional connectedness. Our use of the term really refers to a process whereby parents (for our intended purpose here) have a willingness to openly express and address very sensitive emotions in the most delicate ways. In a practical sense, demonstrating vulnerability means that a parent (or parents) will engage with their adolescent on issues and topics that are highly sensitive . . . It is much easier for parents to make the shift from criticizing their adolescents to comforting them when they are comfortable with expressions of vulnerability. (pp. 183–184)

WE ARE NOT ON THE SAME PAGE

Narrative in Detail

In order to provide a comprehensive picture of when African American couples disagree about child discipline, I will describe one narrative in greater detail. Vashti and Lamont are a compilation of the disciplinary experiences shared by couples who had major parenting disagreements in the study. This case study describes the complexity of this unique parenting situation.

Vashti and Lamont

Vashti, age forty-seven, and Lamont, age forty-nine, have a blended family. This is the second marriage for each of them. They have been married for five years, and each has three children from their previous marriages. Vashti is a high school teacher, and Lamont is head of security at a manufacturing company. Vashti's three children, ages eight, eleven, and fourteen, stay with their father every other weekend. Vashti states that she has a pretty good co-parenting relationship with her ex-husband, and that they at least agree to support child disciplinary decisions at each other's homes. Specifically, if Vashti places one of their children on punishment at her house, the child remains on punishment at her ex-husband's house as well.

Lamont has a flexible co-parenting relationship with his ex-wife, and he can see his children more often than what is stated in the child custody agreement. His ex-wife travels for her job and sometimes needs assistance with childcare when she has to be away for an extended amount of time. He states that he does not have behavioral problems with his children outside of normal "teenage issues." He considers himself a strict disciplinarian, and expects the children in his house to act appropriately.

For the past year, Vashti and Lamont have been having behavioral problems with Vashti's fourteen-year-old son, Ryan, both at school and at home. Her ex-husband has had to address their son's behavior as well, and it began to cause marital problems between Vashti and Lamont. This is what they shared during their interview when asked about their ability to work together as a team in addressing child misbehavior in their home.

Vashti: I think we disagree (about disciplining the kids) most of the time because we're a blended family. I hear both of my biological kids say that Lamont "makes differences." This is especially the case with my son Ryan. He thinks Lamont disciplines him too much and is more harsh than Lamont's biological children. I've seen little things that I don't think is intentional, but I bring things to Lamont's attention. For example, Lamont makes comments in front of the kids that I am more lenient than he is. It is more my style to put my kids on punishment . . . they can't go to a friend house or I take their cell phone for awhile . . . Lamont threatens physical discipline or makes the kids do extra work around the house. Ryan brings this to my attention and sometimes magnifies things and goes overboard with it so I can side with him (my son).

Lamont: How I do things with every kid is different. So, they're gonna be treated differently. I'm not gonna treat every kid the same—like one kid may do something, the punishment may be different for each kid, you know. And I try to explain to my wife that, I am not just singling out Ryan . . . but he does have behavioral issues. My biological children have not had the same problems. I think Ryan has not been held accountable for his actions. Yes, I do come down hard on Ryan sometimes because I am concerned he will jeopardize his future. So, I guess I'm not fair in that sense, but they try to make the point—they try to always make the case, my stepchildren, that I'm more lenient towards my biological kids as opposed to them. They overlook the fact my kids are little older and so I am going to discipline different, but I do not tolerate disrespect . . . not in my house.

Remarks

A common problem in all families are discipline-style differences between mothers and fathers that create family discord. Examples of triangulation (a condition that occurs when a parent forms a coalition with a child that undermines the other parent) were mentioned among couples who disagreed regarding how best to approach child discipline in their families (Margolin et al., 2001). This occurred with blended families as well as couples who were raising their biological children. Participants in the study also cited instances in which the daughter would align with the father while accusing the mother of being too harsh. In either case, the couples expressed anxiety and frustration over this issue.

In blended families, child discipline involving physical punishment can be more complex. Parental authority in child rearing is not automatically provided to stepparents and/or social fathers, particularly when it comes to the use of physical discipline (Ruck, 2008). In most cases, parents can share legal custody, or the court can authorize or delegate parenting to a third party (Ruck, 2008). This is not the same as the village concept of child discipline, where African American communities had an understanding that elders in the community could discipline children that were not their own. The purpose for this shared parenting perspective was to support the child-rearing objectives of the child's parents in their absence, rather than trying to correct or replace them. In the case study, Lamont's desire to change the discipline program of Vashti and her ex-husband could be causing conflict within the overall family system. Lamont represents fathers in this study whose current parenting circumstance threatened their sense of control and/or influence over their children, as they had in their previous marriage or relationship (Johnson & Standford, 2002).

According to scholar and parenting coordinator Dr. Michelle Mitcham (2010), forming a united front as parents and co-parents shows children that they are loved, nurtured, and protected. She has also offered the following tips in order to assist parents who are dealing with separation, high-conflict divorce, or those who are having major parenting differences (Mitcham & Henry, 2007):

1. Do not discuss the adult and court issues such as child support and the contact schedule and other issues about the divorce with the children.
2. If you need someone to lean on, call a friend, pastor, relative, or seek professional help during this difficult time from a mental health professional; not confiding in children.
3. Promote the relevance of the other parent to the child; both parents are the center of the child's life and the child needs a relationship with each. Do not discuss the flaws or shortcomings of the other parent with the child.
4. Do not send messages to other parent through the children.
5. Do not ask your child to keep secrets about their activities at your home; children naturally want to discuss their world with both parents.
6. Allow your children to take their personal belongings with them when they visit the other parent.
7. Allow your children access to other parent (telephone, cell, e-mail) and don't monitor their conversations with the other parent.

8. Communicate through a parent notebook or weekly e-mail to other parent with latest news, school updates, and vacations. (This reduces conflicts and misunderstandings).

9. Attend school functions, celebrations, sports events, and so on and be cordial to the other parent—this teaches your children how to get along despite your differences. It shows them how important they are, and lastly, shows them that even though the love between their parents has changed, the love for them is constant and unwavering (Mitcham, 2010).

REFERENCES

Adkison-Johnson, C., Terpstra, J., Burgos, J., & Payne, D. (2016). African American child discipline: Differences between mothers and fathers. *Family Court Review, 54*(2), 203–220.

Barnes, A. S. (1985). *The Black Middle Class Family*. Bristol, IN: Wyndham Hall Press.

Boyd-Franklin, N. (2003). *Black Families in Therapy: Understanding the African American Experience*. New York, NY: Guilford Press.

Coles, R. L. (2009). *The Best Kept Secret: Single Black Fathers*. Lanham, MD: Rowman & Littlefield.

Coles, R. L., & Green, C. (2010). *The Myth of the Missing Black Father*. New York: Columbia University Press.

Daddis, C., & Smetana, J. (2005). Middle-class African American families' expectations for adolescents' behavioral autonomy. *International Journal of Behavioral Development, 29*, 371–381.

Day, R. D., Peterson, G. W., & McCraken, C. (1998). Predicting spanking on younger and older children by mothers and fathers. *Journal of Marriage and the Family, 60*, 79–94.

Doyle, O., Clark, T., Cryer-Coupet, Q., Nebbitt, V., Goldston, D., Estroff, S., & Magan, I (2015). Unheard voices: African American fathers speak about their parenting practices. *Psychology of Men & Masculinity, 16*(3), 274–283.

Doyle, O., Estroff, S., Goldston, D., Dzirasa, E., Fontes, M., & Burriss, A. (2013). "You gotta have a good help mate": African American fathers' co-parenting experiences. *Psychology of Men & Masculinity, 15*(4), 377–386.

Durodoye, B. (1997). Factors of marital satisfaction among African American couples and Nigerian male/African American female couples. *Journal of Cross-Cultural Psychology, 28*(1), 71–80.

Forehand, R., Parent, J., Golub, A., Reid, M., & Lafko, N. (2015). Involvement in child rearing and firm control parenting by male cohabiting partners in black low-income stepfamilies: Forecasting adolescent problem behaviors. *Behavior Modification, 39*(5), 654–669.

Hamer, J. F. (1997). The fathers of "fatherless" Black children. *Families in Society, 78*(6), 564–578.

Hamer, J. F. (2001). *What It Means To Be Daddy: Fatherhood for Black Men Living Away From Their Children.* New York, NY: Columbia University Press.

Hamer, J. F., & Marchoro, K. (2002). Becoming custodial dads: Exploring parenting among low-income and working-class African American fathers. *Journal of Marriage and Family, 64,* 116–129.

Hardy, K. V., & Laszloffy, T. A. (2005). *Teens Who Hurt: Clinical Interventions to Break the Cycle of Adolescent Violence.* New York: The Guilford Press.

Jackson, A., Choi, J., & Preston, K. (2019). Harsh parenting and Black boys' behavior problems: Single mothers' parenting stress and nonresident fathers' involvement. *Family Relations, 68*(4), 436–449.

Johnson, R. L., & Stanford, P. (2002). *Strength for Their Journey: Five Essential Disciplines African American Parents Must Teach Their Children and Teens.* Harlem Moon: New York.

Jones, S., & Neblett, C. (2019). Black parenting couples' discussions of the racial socialization process: Occurrence and effectiveness. *Journal of Child and Family Studies, 28*(1), 218–232.

Mandara, J., Murray, C., Telesford, J., Varner, F., & Richman, S. (2012). Observed gender differences in African American mother-child relationships and child behavior. *Family Relations, 61*(1), 129–141.

Mandara, J., Varner, F., & Richman, S. (2010). Do African American mothers really "love" their sons and "raise" their daughters? *Journal of Family Psychology, 24*(1), 41–50.

Margolin, G., Godis, E. B., & John, R. S. (2001). Co-parenting: A link between marital conflict and parenting in two-parent families. *Journal of Family Psychology, 15,* 3–21.

Mitcham, M. (2010, April 28). How to be a united front: Co-parenting challenges. *New Pittsburgh Courier Online.* Retrieved from http://www.newpittsburghcourieronline.com

Mitcham-Smith, M., & Henry, W. (2007). High-conflict divorce solutions: Parenting coordination as an innovative co-parenting intervention. *The Family Journal, 15*(4), 368–373.

Nelson, L., Thach, C., Shelton, M., & Boyer, C. (2015). Co-Parenting Relationship Experiences of Black Adolescent Mothers in Active Romantic Partnerships With the Fathers of Their Children. *Journal of Family Nursing, 21*(3), 413–442.

Peters, M. F. (1976). *Nine Black Families: A Study of Household Management and Child Rearing in Black Families with Working Mothers.* Unpublished doctoral dissertation, Harvard University.

Ruck, J. C. (2008). Discipline of stepchildren by stepparents in cases involving joint custody. *Michigan Bar Journal, 87,* p1.

Smetana, J. G. (2000). Middle-class African American adolescents' and parents' conceptions of parental authority and parenting practices: A longitudinal investigation. *Child Development, 71,* 1672–1686.

Smetana, J. G., & Chuang, S. (2001). Middle-class African American parents' conceptions of parenting in early adolescence. *Journal of Research on Adolescence, 11*(2), 177–198.

Smetana, J. G., Daddis, C., & Chuang, S. (2003). "Clean your room!": A longitudinal investigation of adolescent-parent conflict and conflict resolution in middle-class African American families. *Journal of Adolescent Research, 18*(6), 631–650.

Smetana, J. G., & Gaines, C. (1999). Adolescent-parent conflict in middle-class African American families. *Child Development, 70,* 1447–1463.

Stevenson, H. C., Davis, G., & Abdul-Kabir, S. (2001). *Stickin" to, Watchn" Over, and Getting' With: An African American Parent's Guide to Discipline.* San Francisco: Josey Bass.

Vangelisti, A. L. (2004). *The Routledge Handbook of Family Communication.* New York, NY: Routledge.

Chapter 5

Culturally Responsive Service Delivery

Implications for Clinicians and Child Protective Service Workers

Mental health counselors, psychologists, social workers, and other helping professionals play a crucial role in providing guidance to the public and setting policy regarding appropriate child discipline practices. Many of these recommendations and mandates have evolved over time. For example, in a 1976 study of psychologists, most of the research sample spanked or had spanked their own children. Of those who spanked, 70 percent felt that spanking had a positive effect on their children. No psychologist in the study felt that children needed to be spanked often, while three quarters felt children needed to be spanked sometimes. However, Rae and Worchel (1991) found in their study that most pediatric psychologists felt that parents should never spank a child. Similarly, Scheuck et al. (2000) found in their investigation of the corporal punishment beliefs of family, child, and clinical psychologists that 70 percent of participants would never suggest parents spank children, but found it ethical "under rare circumstances." A 2018 study (Miller-Perrin & Rush, 2018) confirmed this position by finding that an overwhelming majority of psychologists (APA members) believed that spanking is a bad disciplinary technique that is harmful to children. This study highlighted a significant shift in the opinion of psychologists over the past three decades.

In 1990, the National Association of Social Workers (NASW), the largest membership organization of professional social workers in the United States adopted an anti-spanking policy because they believed that there were more effective ways to discipline children (Desert, News, 1990). Similarly, a 2006 study (Whitney et al., 2006) of child welfare workers placed spanking at the end of the child discipline continuum. That is, participants viewed methods such as explaining or reasoning with a child as the least restrictive parenting techniques, while threatening to spank or spanking a child was viewed as severe punishment. The majority of participants perceived acts such as hitting a child with straps or belts as abusive.

In 2014, I and several colleagues and students (Jeffrey Terpstra, James Dzikunu Todd Herrenkohl, Keith Alford, and Margaret Sweeney) investigated the perception of professional counselors (members of the American Counseling Association (ACA)) regarding the severity of the disciplinary practices used by parents. I was interested in exploring this topic because little was known at that time about how professional counselors perceived or distinguished child discipline from acts of child abuse. After obtaining human subjects' approval, the ACA membership department supplied our team with a random list of 1,000 professional members. Each participant received the Parental Discipline Practices Scale (PDPS), which was a modified version of the survey that was used in a similar study of social workers by Whitney et al. (2006). The participants consisted of 185 professional counselors who returned a competed survey. The findings are presented in Table 5.1, and frequency distributions and means from a three-point scale (1=either severe nor abusive, 2=severely punishing, or 3=abusive) are provided.

Table 5.1   Summary of Counselors Perception of Child Discipline

Age Group	Neither Severe nor Abusive	Severely Punishing	Abusive	Group Mean	Behavior Mean	P-value
Warning child about consequences of child's behavior						
3 to 5	0.973	0.022	0.005	1.03	1.03	0.9999
6 to 11	0.973	0.022	0.005	1.03		
12 to 14	0.978	0.011	0.011	1.03		
15 to 17	0.978	0.011	0.011	1.03		
Explaining to or reasoning with child						
3 to 5	0.984	0.005	0.011	1.03	1.03	0.9999
6 to 11	0.978	0.011	0.011	1.03		
12 to 14	0.978	0.005	0.016	1.04		
15 to 17	0.978	0.005	0.016	1.04		
Taking some privilege away from child						
3 to 5	0.940	0.044	0.016	1.08	1.06	0.8245
6 to 11	0.951	0.044	0.005	1.05		
12 to 14	0.956	0.038	0.005	1.05		
15 to 17	0.956	0.038	0.005	1.05		
Restricting or grounding child to the house						
3 to 5	0.786	0.181	0.033	1.25	1.15	0.0001
6 to 11	0.895	0.083	0.022	1.13		
12 to 14	0.917	0.072	0.011	1.09		
15 to 17	0.894	0.095	0.011	1.12		
Yelling or shouting at child						
3 to 5	0.175	0.481	0.344	2.17	2.01	0.0001
6 to 11	0.242	0.484	0.275	2.03		
12 to 14	0.302	0.451	0.247	1.95		
15 to 17	0.331	0.448	0.221	1.89		

(Continued)

Table 5.1   Summary of Counselors Perception of Child Discipline (*Continued*)

Age Group	Neither Severe nor Abusive	Severely Punishing	Abusive	Group Mean	Behavior Mean	P-value
Ignoring child (refusing to talk with child)						
3 to 5	0.166	0.331	0.503	2.34	2.16	0.0001
6 to 11	0.199	0.370	0.431	2.23		
12 to 14	0.264	0.433	0.303	2.04		
15 to 17	0.287	0.404	0.309	2.02		
Threatening to spank or hit child						
3 to 5	0.282	0.398	0.320	2.04	2.02	0.5848
6 to 11	0.303	0.382	0.315	2.01		
12 to 14	0.335	0.324	0.341	2.01		
15 to 17	0.322	0.328	0.350	2.03		
Spanking child						
3 to 5	0.158	0.500	0.342	2.18	2.28	0.0001
6 to 11	0.170	0.456	0.374	2.20		
12 to 14	0.139	0.361	0.500	2.36		
15 to 17	0.133	0.343	0.525	2.39		
Ridiculing or making fun of child						
3 to 5	0.016	0.186	0.798	2.78	2.77	0.1263
6 to 11	0.022	0.197	0.781	2.76		
12 to 14	0.017	0.199	0.785	2.77		
15 to 17	0.022	0.203	0.775	2.75		
Telling child that child is no good, stupid						
3 to 5	0.011	0.065	0.924	2.91	2.90	0.0123
6 to 11	0.016	0.071	0.912	2.90		
12 to 14	0.011	0.084	0.905	2.89		
15 to 17	0.017	0.088	0.895	2.88		
Shaking child						
3 to 5	0.000	0.093	0.907	2.91	2.79	0.0001
6 to 11	0.011	0.158	0.831	2.82		
12 to 14	0.022	0.212	0.765	2.74		
15 to 17	0.033	0.232	0.735	2.70		
Slapping child's face						
3 to 5	0.000	0.104	0.896	2.90	2.83	0.0001
6 to 11	0.011	0.115	0.874	2.86		
12 to 14	0.006	0.194	0.800	2.79		
15 to 17	0.011	0.225	0.764	2.75		
Locking child out of the house						
3 to 5	0.000	0.060	0.940	2.94	2.88	0.0001
6 to 11	0.005	0.071	0.923	2.92		
12 to 14	0.006	0.107	0.888	2.88		
15 to 17	0.011	0.215	0.773	2.76		
Hitting child with a fist, punching child						
3 to 5	0.000	0.038	0.962	2.96	2.96	0.9999
6 to 11	0.005	0.038	0.956	2.95		
12 to 14	0.000	0.044	0.956	2.96		
15 to 17	0.000	0.038	0.962	2.96		
Slapping or spanking so as to bruise child						
3 to 5	0.000	0.044	0.956	2.96	2.95	0.4992
6 to 11	0.005	0.044	0.951	2.95		
12 to 14	0.000	0.050	0.950	2.95		
15 to 17	0.000	0.055	0.945	2.95		

(Continued)

Table 5.1   Summary of Counselors Perception of Child Discipline (*Continued*)

Age Group	Neither Severe nor Abusive	Severely Punishing	Abusive	Group Mean	Behavior Mean	P-value
Spanking child with a strap, rope, or belt						
3 to 5	0.011	0.071	0.918	2.91	2.88	0.0327
6 to 11	0.016	0.098	0.885	2.87		
12 to 14	0.006	0.111	0.883	2.88		
15 to 17	0.005	0.110	0.885	2.88		
Burning child, for example, with a cigarette, hot coffee, or a stove						
3 to 5	0.000	0.033	0.967	2.97	2.95	0.3032
6 to 11	0.011	0.044	0.945	2.93		
12 to 14	0.006	0.044	0.950	2.94		
15 to 17	0.005	0.044	0.951	2.95		
Pulling child's hair						
3 to 5	0.000	0.071	0.929	2.93	2.92	0.2844
6 to 11	0.011	0.060	0.929	2.92		
12 to 14	0.006	0.072	0.922	2.92		
15 to 17	0.005	0.077	0.918	2.91		
Threatening to kill child						
3 to 5	0.000	0.033	0.967	2.97	2.96	0.9999
6 to 11	0.005	0.038	0.957	2.95		
12 to 14	0.000	0.034	0.966	2.97		
15 to 17	0.000	0.033	0.967	2.97		

Created by Author.

For example, if we consider the practice of "warning child about consequences of child's behavior" as it pertains to a three-to-five-year-old child, we see that 97.3 percent indicated that this action was neither severely punishing nor abusive, while 2.2 percent and 0.5 percent of the respondents indicated that it was severely punishing or abusive, respectively. It is also notable that "restricting or grounding child to the house," "yelling or shouting at child," and "ignoring child (refusing to talk with child)" are dependent upon the age of the child. For instance, for "restricting or grounding child to the house," the mode response for all four age groups is "neither severe nor abusive." The proportion of counselors perceiving this practice as "neither severe nor abusive" increases from .786 (three-to-five-year-olds) to .894 (fifteen-to-seventeen-year-olds), suggesting that counselors' severity perceptions for this disciplinary practice tend to decrease as the children get older. Regarding "yelling or shouting at child," the mode response for all age groups is "severely punishing," with the proportion of counselors perceiving this disciplinary practice as severely punishing decreasing as children get older. The mode response for the disciplinary technique of "ignoring child (refusing to talk with child)" is "abusive" for three-to-five and six-to-eleven-year-old children, while the mode response for twelve-to-fourteen and fifteen-to-seventeen-year-old children is "severely punishing." This, along with the group means, suggests that counselors' severity perceptions for this particular disciplinary practice tend to decrease as the children get older.

Two disciplinary techniques often associated with physical discipline were also significant when considering the age of the child. In examining the practice of "spanking child," the mode response for three-to-five and six-to-eleven-year-old children is "severely punishing," while the mode response for twelve-to-fourteen and fifteen-to-seventeen-year-old children is "abusive." This, along with the group means, suggests that counselors' severity perceptions for this particular disciplinary practice tend to increase as the children get older. However, unlike "spanking child," "spanking child with a strap, rope, or belt" as a disciplinary method yielded a different result. Specifically, the mode responses for all age groups is "abusive," and the proportion of counselors perceiving this particular disciplinary technique as abusive decreases from .918 (three-to-five-year-old children) to .885 (fifteen-to-seventeen-year-old children).

CULTURALLY RESPONSIVE PRACTICE

A sharper focus on the disciplinary practices of parents has been emerging in social science literature as helping professionals encounter increasingly diverse client families. Over the past twenty years, numerous cultural competence standards have been developed in order to ensure that mental health clinicians and social workers are meeting the needs of a culturally and racially diverse society (Oretga & Coulborn, 2012). For example, Dr. Courtland Lee (2019), a multicultural counseling scholar, defined a *culturally competent counselor* as one who is committed to promoting social justice and engages in counseling practices aimed at challenging inherent inequities in social systems. However, many masters and doctoral training programs in counseling, social work, and psychology do not require systematic training in working specifically with African American clients. As result, African American children and families have been adversely impacted. For instance, Miller, Cahn, and Orellana's (2012) study of child welfare workers, decision makers, and clients noted the lack of rapport that White American child welfare workers had with clients of color, which increased reports, substantiated depositions, and created lengthier stays in foster care. The study also showed that client behavior was taken by workers at face value, and that there was little effort to understand alternative explanations. African American clients stated that cultural gestures or behaviors were interpreted by the child welfare workers as angry or hostile. One participant stated:

> I'm always "hostile" to them (caseworker) because I talk with my hands and my whole body. It's like, where do you see my hostility? I'm not cussing. I'm not picking up things, throwing things. That's hostile to me. If there is a Caucasian person . . . and I move my head like this . . . then I'm threatening them. It is just really ridiculous. (p. 2204)

Regarding child discipline, Fontes (2008) has argued that social service professionals in particular have historically viewed the parenting practices of families of color as abusive. She advocated for the need for social workers and mental health professionals to be competent in their distinctions between functional child discipline and acts of child abuse (Fontes, 2002, 2008). Hill and Crews (2005) also noted that the personal values of counselors related to child discipline may impact the counselor's ability to distinguish appropriate and inappropriate parenting behavior.

PHYSICAL DISCIPLINE VERSUS CHILD ABUSE

I believe that parental use of physical discipline can be constructive in correcting the behavior of children and not be viewed abusive *if* it is used as a last resort option on a child discipline continuum, as illustrated in Figure 5.1.

The automatic presumption advocated by the child welfare system and among mental health professionals that the utilization of physical discipline by parents is problematic in all child- rearing circumstances is ill-advised. Several studies have found that parents with an abusive and violent history spanked their children on average more than non-abusive parents (Barber, 1992; Whipple & Richey, 1997; Whipple & Webster-Stratton, 1991). It should also be acknowledged that a 2019 study (Burke & Doucet, 2019) of

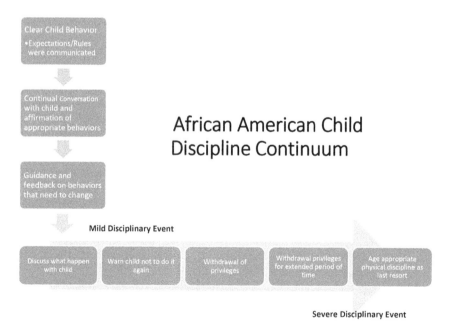

Figure 5.1   African American Child Discipline Continuum. Created by Author.

parental disciplinary practices found that "it is not the disciplinary techniques experienced as a child that impacts how one perceives disciplining their children; rather it is the parental demeanor during discipline that is key" (p. 10) In fact, I had found in my own research and clinical work that African American parents who were troubled by the ways in which they were disciplined as children often refused to use any form of firm discipline with their own children. In contrast, those who were raised in homes where physical discipline was used as a last resort also used this same strategy with their children. These parents often modified different components of their child discipline program dependent on the environmental and cultural changes that affected their families and community.

There is a consensus among researchers that contextual factors should be vigorously weighted in order to fully comprehend various elements of human behavior. For example, studies by Larzelere (1986), Larzelere et al. (2013), and Larzelere et al. (2017) have each found that the context in which corporal punishment occurs can influence the negative impact it can have on children. In order to evaluate whether an African American parent's child discipline crosses the line to abuse, and/or the extent to which modifications should be made to the parent's child-rearing strategies, the following Contextual Child Discipline Guidelines for interviewing or counseling in Figure 5.2 should be considered.

COURT INVOLVEMENT

When a mother's or father's child-rearing practices are called into question due to alleged child abuse, child welfare agencies, attorneys, and judges often turn to clinicians for expert guidance (Budd et al., 2012). Mental health counselors, psychologists, and clinical social workers are often subpoenaed in order to perform this important duty. It is significant, in any case, that clinicians follow the guidelines set forth by their respective Codes of Ethics regarding court evaluations and testimony. Evaluating parenting competencies or providing testimony places the expert in a unique position to shed light on the nature of, and to offer alternative explanations for, disciplinary practices that are not considered mainstream (Budd et al., 2012). The more educated that clinicians are about the child-rearing objectives of African American parents, and corrective actions that they use to accomplish their goals, the more fruitful the alternative explanations can be.

Case Illustration

In order to demonstrate how clinicians or other helping professionals can apply the Contextual Child Discipline Guidelines in their work with African American parents, I will describe in detail the counseling interactions

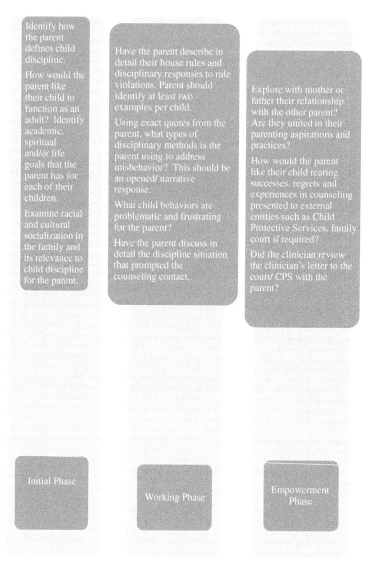

Figure 5.2 Contextual Child Discipline Guidelines. Created by Author.

involving a licensed mental health counselor working with an African American couple. These parents are a compilation of my clinical work with African American mothers and fathers, as well as my consultation activities with child welfare agencies and family court. It should be assumed that informed consent and limits to confidentiality instruction were provided to the parents before their participation in therapy.

William and Janelle Jones sought counseling after child protective services mandated that they change their current parenting practices. Mom is a nurse practitioner, Dad is an electrician, and they live in a large midwestern suburb. Last week, the mother was investigated by child protective services for child abuse. The school counselor informed the principal that Janelle's eight-year-old daughter Jona was "upset" when she came to school that morning. When the school counselor probed further, she found out that Jona's mother had whupped her earlier that morning, and the school counselor noticed a "red area" on her (Jona's) right leg. The school principal called CPS and stated, "I believe Jona is being physically abused at home." Child protective services opened the case for investigation and informed William and Janelle that they could no longer use physical punishment as a disciplinary tool, and also required them to attend anger management classes. In order to gain additional insight, the couple also sought counseling from a seasoned, licensed mental health provider who was not contracted by CPS.

Initial Phase

The first session with William and Janelle was very tense and emotionally charged. Janelle told the counselor when she walked into the room that "if you have a problem with me whuppin my child, we have nothing to talk about. We will find another therapist." William was silent, but glared intensely at the counselor. The counselor thanked the couple for taking the time to meet with her. She made it clear to the couple that her role was to be their therapist, not to monitor for or carry out the recommendations set forth by CPS (Boyd-Franklin & Bry, 2000). At that point, the couple was anxious to tell the counselor exactly what had happened with their daughter, but the counselor calmly stated that she was interested in first hearing about their desires and goals for their child. She assured them they would eventually discuss the disciplinary incident once the counselor got a good grasp of their parenting priorities. Specifically, the counselor wanted to know how they both conceptualized discipline, as well as the types of strategies they used in order to reinforce their values. Janelle felt that it was important that her daughter fulfill her God-given purpose in life. She wanted her to be a self-assured African American woman. William agreed: "I want to make sure she can take care of herself and realize that society is not fair. Unlike her White friends at school, she will have to fight for everything she wants and deserves." The counselor asked what types of strategies they use to address their daughter's behavior, and Janelle stated,

> We usually talk with her first and let her know we expect better from her. Since she was little, she has known how to speak to adults and how she should act in our house. She is at an age where we have taken things away that she likes as a punishment. That seemed to work, but not so much now. I can only remember spanking once when she ran in the grocery parking lot and almost got hit by a

car. That's why this recent event has us both troubled and afraid they will take our daughter away.

Working Phase

The counselor asked the couple to explain in detail how they became involved with CPS. Janelle stated:

> Jona's "tone" with me had started to change. I warned her several times to "watch her mouth" when she is talking to me or her father. That morning before school, I told her to hurry up because she was going to be late for school. She looked me up and down, rolled her eyes, got her books, and started walking out the door. I snatched her up (grabbed her arm and pulled her back in the house) grabbed one of my husband's house shoes and spanked her legs. She started fallen out crying, and I told her to straighten up and get her butt in the car.

William was already at work when it happened, but was fully supportive of his wife's action. He stated, "I just talked to my wife the night before about how we need to be more firm with Jona in correcting her behavior."

Empowerment Phase

Janelle and William were visibly shaken by these recent events. They stated that the police had come to their home later that morning and took Janelle to the police station. William discussed how angry and helpless he felt when he could not protect his wife. Jona was placed with her maternal grandmother until the couple complied with CPS's requirements. The couple hired an attorney to speak on their behalf, knowing that they were dealing with a hostile system. They asked the clinician to write a letter to the court about their time in counseling. The clinician drafted the letter and presented it to the couple for their review, and to see whether they had any concerns before they agreed to sign a release for it to be reviewed outside the counseling session. The counselor also provided child discipline articles and books that reflected the lived experiences of this couple. William and Janelle were very grateful for the information, and Janelle stated she was also going to share these resources with her family and friends.

IMPLICATIONS FOR CULTURALLY RESPONSIVE PRACTICE

The initial contact with African American parents when their disciplinary practices have been questioned, investigated, or criminalized can be very tense and emotionally charged. The anger and distrust often expressed by African American mothers and fathers with CPS and mental health clinicians have been viewed by social scientists as an appropriate response to a state agency that has historically disrupted, restructured, and policed African American families (Adkison-Johnson & Johnson, 2019; Boyd-Franklin, 2003; Roberts, 2002, 2014). In order to minimize distrust, helping professionals should demonstrate that they comprehend the context of anger and should articulate a clear alliance with their clients. It has been my experience as a professor in counselor education and a clinical mental health counseling supervisor that these particular therapeutic occurrences are best handled by more advanced clinicians, principally those who have clarified their own child discipline perspectives and are most interested in meeting the child-rearing goals of the parents, as opposed to changing them. I have too often witnessed limited or newly licensed mental health providers remark in family court proceedings on the "resistance" of African American mothers and fathers to change, rather than their non-compliance being clarified with regard to the circumstance that brought them to counseling while negotiating a mental health and/or social service system that is unsuited to straightforwardly address African American concerns.

During the working phase, the concrete details of the couples' present-ing situation are revealed. Utilizing questions contained in the Contextual Child Discipline Guidelines can assist in obtaining a comprehensive view of the disciplinary event. Like all clients who enter counseling, William and Janelle should be informed of the limits of confidentiality, particularly when explaining the counselor's role in reporting suspected child abuse to child protective services. Encouraging the couple to engage in an open and honest dialogue about their disciplinary practices is likely to invite them to describe events that may place the counselor in a precarious position as a mandated reporter (Adkison-Johnson, 2015). It is important to keep in mind that it is not against the law to use physical discipline as a method to parent children. State laws have different approaches in addressing child discipline, and the most common approach used in a majority of states maintain that parents may use reasonable force to discipline a child (Laird, 2015). However, in the event that a parent discloses an act of suspected child abuse, the counselor is legally bound to report such acts to child protective services for further investigation. In order to protect the counseling rights of both William and Janelle, each parent should fully understand the limits of confidentiality before agreeing to share disciplinary information. It is equally important to assume that like all competent parents, African American mothers and fathers are trying their best to rear their children properly. This affirming perspective can facilitate an atmosphere of trust and respect for African American parents, encouraging them to share their experiences.

The empowerment phase of the counseling process is critical, given that parents must interact with the court and child protective services in order to regain custody of their children. The counselor can be instrumental in terms of helping to empower parents to have meaningful and purposeful engagement with social workers and the family court. According to Dr. Nancy Boyd-Franklin (2003), prominent African American family therapist and scholar:

> *Empowerment* is defined as the process whereby the therapist restructures the family to facilitate the appropriate designation and use of power within the family system and to mobilize the family's ability to successfully interact with external systems . . . Empowerment often involves helping parents to take back control of their families and feel that they can effect important changes for themselves. This is very threatening to many family therapists because it often requires them to take a stand vis-à-vis a decision made by another agency, thus forcing them to abandon their stances of "neutrality" in therapy . . . forces the therapist to examine his or her own values and political, cultural, and religious beliefs and biases, and to intervene accordingly. It is through this examination and the therapist's ability to convey respect for the families she or he treats that the therapist creates an atmosphere in which empowerment can occur. (pp. 26–27)

Assisting parents with clearly articulating their parenting goals and the range of disciplinary strategies they use with their children will help them demonstrate to the court that they are competent parents. Discussing additional resources, such as making sure they have culturally competent legal representation while dealing with CPS, can also empower both parents as well.

CONCLUDING REMARKS

It is important to emphasize that child abuse is very real and occurs in African American families as it can in all kinds of families. Just because African American parents utilize physical discipline should not automatically rule out that the parent has the potential to apply this strategy in an abusive manner. There has and will be African American parents who carelessly or arbitrarily use physical discipline with their children, which should be viewed as a form of child abuse. Other forms of child abuse, such as emotional abuse and neglect, are also areas that should be evaluated when applying Contextual Child Discipline Guidelines. Consequently, there is a pressing need for policymakers and researchers to develop more appropriate child discipline protocols for their workers to accurately identify child abuse in African American families. Moreover, when whether or not a parent uses physical discipline is the primary lens to determine appropriate parenting behavior, real cases of abuse may go unrecognized. Thus, it is important that helping professionals facilitate competent, culturally responsive direction with African American mothers and fathers. This particular type of service delivery will help professionals to distinguish between African American families that are using appropriate discipline from those whose disciplinary practices are putting their children at risk of being abused.

REFERENCES

Adkison-Bradley, C. (2011). Seeing African American mothers and fathers as competent parents: Implications for counselor education research and practice. *The Family Journal, 19*, 307–313.

Adkison-Bradley, C., Terpstra, J., & Dormitorio, B. (2014). Child discipline in African American families: A study of patterns and context. *The Family Journal: Counseling and Therapy for Couples and Families, 22*(2), 198–205.

Adkison-Johnson, C. (2015). Child discipline and African American parents with adolescent children: A psycho-educational approach to clinical mental health counseling. *Journal of Mental Health Counseling, 37*(3), 221–233.

American Counseling Association (ACA). (2014). *Code of Ethics*. Alexandria, VA: American Counseling Association.

American Mental Health Counseling Association. (2010). *Standards for the Practice of Mental Health Counseling*. Alexandria, VA: AMHCA.

Belgrave, F. Z., & Allison, K. W. (2010). *African American Psychology: From Africa to. America*. Los Angeles, CA: Sage.

Boyd-Franklin, N. (2003). *Black Families in Therapy: Understanding the African American Experience*. New York, NY: Guilford Press.

Bradley, C. (1998). Child rearing in African American families: A study of disciplinary methods used by African American parents. *Journal of Multicultural Counseling and Development, 26*, 273–281.

Bradley, C. (2000). The disciplinary practices of African American fathers: A closer look. *Journal of African American Men, 5*, 43–61.

Budd, K. S., Clark, J., & Cornell, M. A. (2011). *Evaluation of Parenting Capacity in Child Protection*. New York, NY: Oxford University Press.

Burke, J. L., & Doucet, J. M. (2019). Deciding on discipline: The importance of parent demeanor in the transmission of discipline practices. *Social Sciences, 8*, 95. doi: 10.3390/socsci8030095

Day, R. D., Peterson, G. W., & McCraken, C. (1998). Predicting spanking on younger and older children by mothers and fathers. *Journal of Marriage and the Family, 60*, 79–94.

Desert News. (1990). *Social Workers Advise Parents Not to Spank*. https://www.deseret.com/1990/8/25/18878032/social-workers-advise-parents-not-to-spank-br

Fontes, L. A. (2002). Child discipline and physical abuse in immigrant Latino families: Reducing violence and misunderstandings. *Journal of Counseling and Development, 80*, 31–40.

Fontes, L. A. (2008). *Child Abuse and Culture: Working with Diverse Families.* New York: Guilford Press.

Gray, S. S., & Nybell, L. M. (1990). Issues in African-American family preservation. *Child Welfare, 69*(6), 513–523.

Greene, K., & Garner, P. (2012). African American mothers' disciplinary responses: Associations with family background characteristics, maternal childrearing attitudes, and child manageability. *Journal of Family Economic Issues, 33*, 400–409.

Henderson, K. L. (2013). Mandated reporting of child abuse: considerations and guidelines for mental health counselors. *Journal of Mental Health Counseling, 35*(4), 269–309.

Kriz, K., & Skivenes, M. (2011). How child welfare workers view their work with racial and ethnic minority families: The United States in contrast to England and Norway. *Children and Youth Services Review, 33*, 1866–1874.

Laird, L. (April, 2015). Experts debate line between spanking and abuse. *American Bar Association Journal, 60*, 65.

Lansford, J. E., Wager, L. B., Bates, J. E. Dodge, K. A., & Pettit, G. S. (2012). Parental reasoning, denying privileges, yelling and spanking: Ethnic differences and associations with child externalizing behavior. *Parenting: Science and Practice, 12*, 42–56.

Larzelere, R. E. (1986). Moderate spanking: Model or deterrent of children's aggression in the family? *Journal of Family Violence, 1*, 27–35.

Larzelere, R. E., Cox, R. B., Jr., & Mandara, J. (2013). Responding to misbehavior in young children: How authoritative parents enhance reasoning with firm control. In R. E. Larzelere, A. S. Morris & A. W. Harrist (Eds.), *Authoritative Parenting: Synthesizing Nurturance and Discipline for Optimal Child Development* (pp. 89–111). Washington, DC: American Psychological Association Press.

Larzelere, R. E., Knowles, S. J., Henry, C. S., & Ritchie, K. L. (2018). Immediate and long-term effectiveness of disciplinary tactics by type of toddler noncompliance. *Parenting: Science & Practice, 18*, 141–171. doi: 10.1080/15295192.2018.1465304

Larzelere, R. E., Morris, A. S., & Harrist, A. W. (Eds.). (2013). *Authoritative Parenting: Synthesizing Nurturance and Discipline for Optimal Child Development.* Washington, DC: American Psychological Association Press. http://www.apa.org/pubs/books/4318109.aspx

Lee, C. (2019). *Multicultural Issues in Counseling: New Approaches to Diversity* (Courtland C. Lee Ed.; 5th Ed.). Alexandria, VA: American Counseling Association.

Margolin, G., Godis, E. B., & John, R. S. (2001). Co-parenting: A link between marital conflict and parenting in two-parent families. *Journal of Family Psychology, 15*, 3–21.

McLoyd, V. C., & Smith, J. (2002). Physical discipline and behavior problems in African American, European American, and Hispanic Children: Emotional support as a moderator. *Journal of Marriage and Family, 64*(1), 40–53.

McKinney, C., Milone, M. C., & Renk, K. (2011). Parenting and late adolescent emotional adjustment: Mediating effects of discipline and gender. *Child Psychiatry and Human Development, 42*, 463–481.

Miller, K., Cahn, K., & Orellana, E. (2012). Dynamics that contribute to racial disproportionality and disparity: Perspectives from child welfare professionals, community partners, and families. *Children and Youth Services Review, 34*(11), 2201–2207.

Miller-Perrin, C., & Rush, R. (2018). Attitudes, knowledge, practices, and ethical beliefs of psychologists related to spanking: A survey of American psychological association division members. *Psychology, Public Policy, and Law, 24*(4), 405–417.

National Association of Social Workers. (2000). *Social Work Speaks; Policy Statements'* (5th ed.). Washington, DC: NASW Press.

Ortega, R., & Faller, K. (2011). Training child welfare workers from an intersectional cultural humility perspective: A paradigm shift. *Child Welfare, 90*(5), 27–49.

Patrick, R. B., & Gibbs, J. C. (2012). Inductive discipline, parental expression of disappointed expectations, and moral identity in adolescence. *Journal of Youth and Adolescence, 41*, 973–983.

Rae, W. A., & Worchel, F. F. (1991). Ethical beliefs and behaviors of pediatric psychologists: A survey. *Journal of Pediatric Psychology, 16*, 727–745.

Roberts, D. (2002). *Shattered Bonds: The Color of Child Welfare*. New York, NY: Basic Books.

Roberts, D. (2012). Prison, foster care, and the systemic punishment of Black mothers. *UCLA Law Review, 59*, 1474–1504.

Scheuck, E. R., Lyman, R. D., & Bodin, S. D. (2000). Ethical beliefs, attitudes, and professional practices of psychologists regarding parental use of corporal punishment: A survey. *Children's Services: Social Policy, Research and Practice, 3*(1), 23–38.

Sheehan, M. J., & Watson, M. W. (2008). Reciprocal influences between maternal discipline techniques and aggression in children and adolescents. *Aggressive Behvaior, 34*, 245–255.

Stevenson, H. C., Davis, G., & Abdul-Kabir, S. (2001). *Stickin' to, Watchin' Over, and Getting' With: An African American Parent's Guide to Discipline*. Jossey-Bass: San Francisco.

Straus, M. A., Douglas, E. M., & Medeiros, R. A. (2014). *The Primordial Violence: Spanking Children, Psychological Development, Violence and Crime*. New York and London: Routledge.

Taylor, C. A., Fleckman, J. M., Scholer, S., & Nelson, B (2018). US pediatricians' attitudes, beliefs, and perceived injunctive norms about spanking. *Journal of Developmental and Behavioral Pediatrics, 39*(7), 564–572

Whipple, E. E., Fitzgerald, H. E., & Zucker, R. A. (1995). Parent-child interactions in alcoholic and nonalcoholic families. *American Journal of Orthopsychiatry, 65*, 153–159.

Whipple, E. E., & Richey, C. (1997). Crossing the line from physical discipline to child abuse: How much is too much? *Child Abuse & Neglect, 21*(5), 431–444.

Whipple, E. E., & Webster-Stratton, C. (1991). The role of parental stress in physically abusive families. *Child Abuse & Neglect, 15*, 279–291.

Whipple E. E., & Wilson, S. R. (1996). Evaluation of a parent education program for families at risk of physical child abuse. *Families in Society, 77*, 227–239.

Whitney, S. D., Tajima, E. A., Herrenkohl, T. I., & Huang, B. (2006). Defining child abuse: Exploring variations in ratings of discipline severity among child welfare practitioners. *Child and Adolescent Social Work Journal, 23*(3), 316–342.

Wilson, C., & Leung, S. (2006). Maternal attributions and observed maternal behavior: Are they linked? *Behavioral and Cognitive Psychotherapy, 35*, 165–178.

Yabko, B. A., Hokoda, A., & Ulloa, E (2008). Depression as a mediator between family factors and peer-bullying victimization in Latino adolescents. *Violence and Victims, 23*(6), 727–742.

Yoos, H. L., Kitzman, H., Olds, D. L., & Overacker, I. (1995). Child rearing beliefs in the African–American community: Implications for culturally competent pediatric care. *Journal of Pediatric Nursing, 10*(6), 343–352.

Chapter 6

Addressing Child Discipline in Court

Perspective from a Trial Lawyer

E. Dorphine Payne, JD

The manner in which a parent disciplines their children is one of the court's most important considerations in determining criminal liability, custody, placement, cases of abuse and/or neglect, or the termination of parental rights. The court must of course be directed by the law and the facts of each case. Every individual involved, including the judge, lawyer, police officer, caseworker, experts, and service provider in both criminal and family court matters, brings in their own biases and assumptions into the case. Those biases can affect whether or not an individual is charged criminally or civilly; determine placement and/or custody; and influence the possible termination of parental rights. Much of this can be impacted by an attorney's approach to the representation of his/her client.

Cases that are particularly difficult are those that require representation in both criminal and family courts, such as child discipline cases. In family court, these cases would generally fall under a Child Abuse and Neglect statute MCL722.622(2) (G, K, I) defined as:

(G) "Child abuse" means harm or threatened harm to a child's health or welfare that occurs through nonaccidental physical or mental injury, sexual abuse, sexual exploitation, or maltreatment, by a parent, a legal guardian, or any other person responsible for the child's health or welfare or by a teacher, a teacher's aide, or a member of the clergy.

(K) "Child neglect" means harm or threatened harm to a child's health or welfare by a parent, legal guardian, or any other person responsible for the child's health or welfare that occurs through either of the following:

(I) Negligent treatment, including the failure to provide adequate food, clothing, shelter, or medical care, though financially able to do so, or by the failure to seek financial or other reasonable means to provide adequate food, clothing, shelter, or medical care.

The focus of this chapter will be on what I've learned in representing and how I defend cases involving African American clients versus White American clients concerning child discipline. I will be referring to some actual cited cases, as well as a compilation of cases that I have personally handled. I will use pseudonyms to avoid easy recognition of the actual case in order to risk offending or embarrassing the clients I have represented in the past.

GENERAL INFORMATION

Some cases are easier to work through than others, particularly those involving outright torture and extreme physical abuse of a child versus difficult ones that involve simply spanking a child in the presence of Child Protective Services (CPS). The former is usually handled criminally first, and then resolved in family court. If exonerated in criminal court, the family court can dismiss a CPS case depending upon the circumstances.

Whether in criminal or family court, attorneys must factor in a myriad of considerations in preparing a case. Primarily, we must protect the rights of the clients who we represent. The first among those rights are the basic presumptions provided by the U.S. Constitution. In family court, it is the presumption of fitness, and in criminal court, it is the presumption of innocence. Of course, among our considerations are who did or did not correctly interpret those presumptions prior to receiving the case, that is, police, Child Protective Services investigators, and prosecutors, as well as managing how the next level of involved individuals will be weighing in, including experts, evaluators, assessors, and eventually the judge and/or jury. If the client is African American, understanding that there will be bias along the way, the attorney should keep a watchful eye on how those individuals arrive at their findings. Most importantly, looking through a racial/cultural lens provides the client with the greatest opportunity to level the field.

Explicit bias is easier to address than implicit systemic bias. Dr. Martin Luther King could challenge legal inequities in the South because Jim Crow laws were on the books and racism was advertised by "no coloreds allowed" signs outside restaurants and hotels, as well as on buses directing Negros to the back. Those signs were not as prevalent in the North, but we knew where we could and could not be served. The only way to challenge in the North was to sit down in the restaurant, wait for someone to either invite you to leave or refuse to serve you, and then publicly demonstrate. To anyone other than those who are slighted, the bias would go unnoticed. And although the signs have been taken down by now, change has been slow or halted altogether as the system continues to reinvent ways in which to quietly perpetuate racial discrimination.

It is imperative that those of us involved in the legal system understand that African Americans are still considered violent people for no apparent reason, as well as understanding that this insight legally impacts the fair treatment of the clients who we represent. In so doing, we must recognize that the following does not apply to African American parents.

The Supreme Court has stated that there is a presumption that fit parents act in their children's best interests, *Parham v. J. R.*, 442 U. S. 584, 602:

- There is normally no reason or compelling interest for the state to inject itself into the private realm of the family to further question fit parents' ability to make the best decisions regarding their children. *Reno v. Flores*, 507 U. S. 292, 304.
- The state may not interfere in child-rearing decisions when a fit parent is available. *Troxel v. Granville*, 530 U.S. 57 (2000).

African American parents know that these presumptions don't apply to them. Policies can be our enemy, because they can be applied indiscriminately and used as an excuse to make inequitable decisions. These policies also provide a shield of deniability for the decision-maker to say that "it's per policy." I've found that uniformity in the law is a defense attorney's best friend.

BEST INTEREST FACTORS

When considering domestic cases (divorce, child custody, and parenting time), everyone involved, including the plaintiff's attorney, defendant's attorney, judge, therapist, and parent evaluator, must understand that the ultimate decision will be based upon the Best Interest Factors (hereafter BIF). Therefore, both sides must analyze and strategize around those factors. As the case develops, therapists and parent evaluations are all based upon the same factors. Finally, at trial, the case will be presented and the court will decide by weighing evidence presented by the parties relative to the following BIF (MCL 722, 23). These factors are not policy; rather, they are statutory:

As used in this act, "best interests of the child" means the sum total of the following factors to be considered, evaluated, and determined by the court:

(a) The love, affection, and other emotional ties existing between the parties involved and the child.

(b) The capacity and disposition of the parties involved to give the child love, affection, and guidance and to continue the education and raising of the child in his or her religion or creed, if any.

(c) The capacity and disposition of the parties involved to provide the child with food, clothing, medical care or other remedial care recognized and permitted under the laws of this state in place of medical care, and other material needs.

(d) The length of time the child has lived in a stable, satisfactory environment, and the desirability of maintaining continuity.

(e) The permanence, as a family unit, of the existing or proposed custodial home or homes.

(f) The moral fitness of the parties involved.

(g) The mental and physical health of the parties involved.

(h) The home, school, and community record of the child.

(i) The reasonable preference of the child, if the court considers the child to be of sufficient age to express preference.

(j) The willingness and ability of each of the parties to facilitate and encourage a close and continuing parent-child relationship between the child and the other parent or the child and the parents. A court may not consider negatively for the purposes of this factor any reasonable action taken by a parent to protect a child or that parent from sexual assault or domestic violence by the child's other parent.

(k) Domestic violence, regardless of whether the violence was directed against or witnessed by the child.

(l) Any other factor considered by the court to be relevant to a particular child custody dispute.

Although perfect on paper, I do not purport that the usage of these factors eliminates structural racism. However, uniformity does provide an opportunity to mitigate bias. It is important for attorneys to understand how the judge may weigh one factor more heavily than another in making decisions about custody or parenting time. For example, one of the Best Interest Factors in considering parenting time is Factor B. One of the questions begged relating to guidance is: Which parent has the greater capacity to discipline the child? The opposition may offer evidence that your client uses physical discipline. The court's knee-jerk reaction may be "spanking is abuse per se," leading the judge to consider physical discipline as abusive and weigh it under Factor J or K (domestic violence) or Factor M (morally unfit) rather than Factor B (guidance and discipline) (most attorneys either know by experience or have researched how a particular judge evaluates BIFs). In that instance, the advantage of BIFs is that the attorney has an opportunity to present his case and provide pertinent evidence in order to dissuade the "knee jerk reaction," or challenge the other side's allegations of improper discipline by delving deeper into how the parent arrives at administering physical discipline. The major issue here is that not everyone is on the same page when examining that process.

DISCIPLINARY BEST PRACTICE FACTORS

In CPS cases, African American parents who whup their children are frequently labeled "out of control" or violent, and without more information are considered to be incompetent parents. Courts will order that they engage in parenting classes in order to address this lack. Some judges consider CPS investigators to be experts on parenting, when many of these workers are in fact entry-level professionals. They therefore would have neither the broad range of experience nor enough information with which to evaluate parenting skills. They would just have to operate "per policy." Unfortunately, the children are often removed, or the parent is ordered out of the house for six months to a year, before the issue can be properly tried before the court.

As an attorney who has experienced this phenomenon many times, I have developed a method to use when I eventually got to trial to rebut the presumption that African American mothers and fathers are reckless parents. I call it the Disciplinary Best Practices Factors (hereafter DBPF), and its uniformity assists a biased system in order to equitably maneuver through the complexity of child discipline decisions (Adkison-Johnson et al., 2016).

Disciplinary Best Practice Factors (DBPF)

A. *Context:* Used when disciplining the child? What happened that led up to the event?

B. *Parenting style Determination:* range of discipline used by the parent. Is there a continuum: what are the disciplinary techniques in your arsenal? When and under what circumstances are they employed?

C. *Informational piece* that accompanies physical discipline? Do you explain "why" to the child? At what point is the information provided: before, during, after, or a combination?

D. *Clearly Defined Expectations and Consequences are Communicated:* Child understands what is and is not appropriate behavior and forewarned about the consequences. For example, "If you do this, you will lose your privileges. If you do that, the punishment will be more severe."

E. *Two parents—1 child—2 different parenting styles:* How does a father/mother see what he/she does differently than what the other parent is doing? Do the children use it to their advantage?

F. *Complimentary methods of discipline:* Whether rearing children in the same household or separately, are the two methods of discipline complementary to one another (i.e., mother loving her son and raising her daughter; father loving his daughter and raising his son)?

G. *Goals:* What are the parenting goals for the child; that is, how does the parent want to see the child as an adult?

H. *Goal Attainment Plan:* How does she intend to reach these goals and/or how does his discipline play into attaining the goals?

I. *Injury:* Was the child injured; if so, what was the extent of the injury?

J. *Causation:* Was the injury a direct or indirect cause of the parent's actions?

K. *Outcomes (positive or negative):* What were the results of your disciplinary techniques?

DBPF tend to humanize people who are otherwise dehumanized by the system. There are parents who may respond to "what happened" with "I just pop them when they get out of line." No continuum or informational piece, just "I pop em." This helps a decision-maker to quickly draw the conclusion that this parent needs some parenting skill development. Clearly, this individual doesn't know what he doesn't know. I have had similar conversations with very young client/parents as well; however rare, they can be disturbing. But for the most part, that has not been my experience. Most of the time, if you go through the DBPF with a parent, he/she can answer the questions indicating the differing levels of insight and methodology in discipline.

Twenty years ago, CPS in my county took the extremely hard line of zero tolerance. If the child was spanked, it was abuse per se, and the case was brought to court. The belief was that mental injury followed any physical altercation.

Injury is certainly relevant, but in my county, "0 tolerance" was exercised to the extreme. The child could have been injured physically or emotionally, and considered injury during the threat of a whupping sufficient grounds for action. The following two cases illustrate my position:

Case #1. Minor broke her collar bone when a parent threatened to spank her. She was attempting to escape a spanking. While running from her mother, she ran into a couch, tripped, fell into the coffee table, and broke her collar bone. The parent never touched the child. The next morning, when the parent realized how much pain her daughter was in, she took the child to the ER. Upon ascertaining the facts of the case ("I was scared I was gonna get a whupppin"), the doctor filed a report with CPS.

Subsequently, CPS hauled the parent into court, alleging child abuse/physical discipline resulting in an injury. The child and her siblings were removed and placed in foster care. Context and continuum matter. At trial, the testimony of the child was that she had lied to her mother for months about her math class. Her mother continually inquired about math, because it was a difficult subject for her. She had told her mother that she was doing well, had gotten a tutor, and was getting an "A." At the first grading period, knowing that her grade was actually an "F," she told her teachers that she was going to be in trouble because her mother hated lying and highly valued her education. She knew she would get a whuppin. She further testified that her mother usually punished her by taking away her phone or restricting her television time. She also grounded her from attending social events. She further testified that she knew this would be different because her mom valued honesty and education. The interesting point in the case was that CPS attempted to paint the mother as "volatile," and that the teachers were "fearful" of her always coming to the school and "demanding" services for her daughter. The middle school principal testified about the "involvement" and "passion" displayed by the parent about her daughter's education. The principal waxed eloquently on the stand when he corrected the terminology used, and said that she was no different than any other "helicopter parent." The court found in favor of the mother, returned the children, and dismissed the case.

Case #2. The parent used the continuum, and the final blow was a physical strike. A mother spanked her son when he refused to go to school. She had tried time outs, taking away his toys and his electronics, making him sit in his room, not allowing him to go out and play soccer or hockey, not allowing him to skate board or ride his bike, all to no avail. The last morning, when he said he wasn't going to school, she said, "Okay," then went upstairs, retrieved a belt, came back downstairs, and proceeded to whup him on top of his clothes. Like most eleven-year-old boys, he was wearing jeans and a sweat shirt at the time.

Following the spanking, he got up and went to school and reported the incident to school personnel, who in turn reported it to CPS. CPS took the minor to the doctor and discovered that there was some bruising on the child's legs. The mother was hauled into court. The court removed her son and daughter because she would not agree to the "safety plan." At trial, we advanced three arguments and one defense to the injury. Her primary argument was fundamental and constitutional, that is, her rights to rear her children the way she saw fit, and if a spanking were necessary, she should be able to do it. Her secondary argument was a continuum/and success: that she had a good reason to spank him after trying everything else that didn't work. Spanking was the last resort in her case. The former did not work; the latter did—he subsequently went to school. Her tertiary argument was that if she failed to get her child to school, she would risk being charged with educational neglect. The defense was that he had played hockey and skateboarded, and the positions of the injuries were more consistent with those activities than spanking him over his clothes (a fact undisputed by the prosecutor). Subsequently, at trial, the court agreed.

We prevailed in both cases; however, there was a difference in how one case was handled over the other. The first mother was African American, and the second was White American. Some interesting comparisons can be found between the two cases. We won both cases, we tried both cases in front of the same judge, and we used the same expert witness; both parents used a continuum when disciplining their child.

In contrast, in Case #1, labeling is important. The caseworkers and prosecutor used words such as "volatile," "out of control," and "fearful," demanding to persuade the judge that she was almost an animal, not just in the home but in the community and at the school as well. Those labels conjured up a far different picture than the words "passionate," "educationally focused," "helicopter mom," and "fierce advocate" that were used by the principal when describing the mother. The mother and the principal were both African American, and the prosecutor used language to make her appear more like an animal, acting out of impulse. My immediate job was to build the presumption that this mother was a human being who was a fit parent. The next step was to fight the fact that she had done something wrong.

In Case #2, no such imagery was used. The focus was simply on the fact that she had spanked her son and purportedly caused injury. This case was easier to work than the first one, because we started with the presumption that she was a fit parent but had spanked her child and caused injury.

After prevailing in court over a period of time, CPS only brought cases into court when the child was injured while being physically disciplined.

IMPACT POLICY—EVEN THE PLAYING FIELD

Just as is the case with Best Interest Factors, if DBPF were law, it would more clearly define the differences between discipline and abuse when physical discipline is applied. By utilizing a uniform set of disciplinary guidelines when making decisions about whether whuppins are discipline versus abuse, it would impact Department of Health and Human Service Policy regarding physical discipline. Finally, it could also restore the presumption that African American parents are fit, even if they use physical discipline.

This uniformity may be a valuable tool for CPS investigators when deciding about whether or not a child has been abused. It has already altered the ways that they do business in my community. Twenty years ago, CPS brought any case that involved physical discipline into court. After winning cases in my county, I was excited that we had impacted the policy, because CPS now brings physical discipline cases into court that involve injury to the child, with only a few exceptions.

This may appear to be a positive change on its face, but careful scrutiny reveals a policy that is both insidious and even more harmful to the parent than before. Currently, instead of taking a case for physical discipline into court, the DHHS opens informal cases. This involves the family attending a Family Team Meeting, at which the parents sign and cooperate with a Service Agreement and Safety Plan. That Agreement usually mandates parenting classes, psychological evaluation, therapy, and refraining from using physical discipline. The parents sign under the threat that they will be taken to court if they do not. This is all done without the advice of counsel. No one explains to them that whether they cooperate informally or not, they can be placed on the Central Registry, indicating that they are substantiated for child abuse without due process. No one warns them that the information on that Central Registry is accessible to a future employer or school official. No one helps them understand its potential impact on their ability to earn a living or participate in their child's school functions (SOM DHHS, CPS, Child Abuse and Neglect Central Registry PSM 713-13, p. 6). DHHS sends them a letter after the fact informing them that their names have been placed on the perpetrator registry of the Central Registry (State of Michigan DHHS Children's Protective Services Manual, CPS Legal Requirements, CSM 7114-4, p. 8). At that point, they are not entitled to an indigent defense attorney. The formal route assures them the right to council, and if they go to court and prevail, they can be removed from that registry at the local level.

The consequences are far-reaching, and almost impossible to overcome. The Expunction process is arduous, complex, and expensive. It requires a parent to file an appeal and adjudicate the case before an Administrative Law Judge. Opposing counsel is the Attorney General's Office. And even if the parent is fortunate enough to win the case, the ALJ's order is a recommended order to expunge. But DHHS can refuse, and the parent must then appeal to the Circuit Court of original jurisdiction (SOM DHHS CPS Manual, Amendment or Expunction, PSM 717-2, p. 1). This will require that he order and purchase the trial transcript, which can be thousands of dollars, depending upon the length of the ALJ trial, and then file the appeal. Most parents have neither the skill nor the finances to persist. Most cannot afford an attorney.

CASE IN DETAIL

Below, I have provided a detailed description of my process when establishing the presumption that my client is a fit parent. I have used the Work the

Work the Case Model

Figure 6.1   **Work the Case Model.** Created by Author.

Case model (see Figure 6.1) for most of my work for African American parents when their disciplinary practices have been challenged.

CULTIVATE RELATIONSHIP TO DEVELOP:
RESPECT, DIGNITY, AND TRUST

I have found that in many instances, it is easier to represent White American clients than African American clients, relative to being able to get better plea agreements, judgments, mercy, sentencing, and related dispositions. Interestingly, I've found that no matter the race of the client, my own color could invoke sometimes more confidence and other times less confidence in my legal ability. I have experienced clients of both races ask for another attorney (or want to) based upon the color of *my* skin. The fact that I am available to represent them should at least allow me the presumption that I am a bar-certified practicing attorney. However, I readily point with pride to my Notre Dame Law Degree in order to challenge their racial assumptions. After our first court appearance and/or opportunity to talk, they quickly change their minds, not because they are impressed by the ND Law Degree, but because I like to fight. And no matter what culture or race, clients want someone whom they believe to be in the yoke with them. Gaining the client's confidence is my first action plan in cultivating a relationship.

After helping a client understand that I cannot guarantee outcomes, but that I can certainly guarantee that I will fight for them, I move on to cultivating the relationship by demonstrating to my client that there will be respect, dignity, and trust between us. Many indigent attorneys only meet with their clients prior to a court hearing. In some cases I do the same, but many times, especially if I'm preparing for trial, I invite clients to meet with me at my office. That gesture provides an opportunity to demonstrate that I respect the client and that the case is important to me. Other non-verbal cues during the initial visit, that is, meeting in my conference room, include offering the client a beverage, and then breaking the ice during cordial conversation by sharing something about myself, opening doors for mutual respect and trust. Conversations regarding expectations also lay the groundwork for how our working relationship will proceed. And finally, I practice active listening.

EXTENSIVE INTERVIEW QUESTIONS FOR CLIENT

My interview questions are probably more in-depth than those that most indigent attorney–client relationships ask. That is why we work to develop trust, because the client needs to be able to relax and tell me what we need to know in order to have any possibility of success in court. Time is a real commitment. Background information about my client provides insight into and assists in developing trial strategy, such as how to frame questions that will humanize the client to the court, whether or not I want to put my client on the witness stand, and how to direct my client or allow the prosecutor to call the client to the stand so that I can cross-examine or lead him. Most importantly, it diminishes the element of surprise in terms of responses to questions while on the witness stand. Family history is extremely important in discovering what makes an individual tick. For example, hearing about his parents and who the primary caregiver was in his life, as well as the level and manner of his engagement with his parent(s), can show me how he came to think the way he does. Questions about how he was disciplined as a child, and more importantly how he felt about it, are very important as well. I don't want to hear a prosecutor elicit testimony that his mother whupped him and that he considered it to be abusive. Socioeconomic background and parents' educational background, along with their level of trust in various systems, all inform me about the development of a client's own core principles.

Discover How Answers to the Prior Questions Translate into the Client's Current Family Dynamic

A household's core principles dictate what is important regarding a parent rearing his or her children. I ask questions about the client's vision for the future they see for their family and children. What are their hopes and dreams? What are their fears and concerns? It is also important to know whether or not and how they communicate these hopes, dreams, and values to their children. Finally, we get to the methods of discipline and corrective measures employed in the household, and whether they are the same or similar to those used by the client's own parents during childhood.

Establish the Current Family's Discipline Protocol

In all excessive discipline cases, the most important information is the family's discipline protocol, especially when working with African American parents. We must establish what happens when a child misbehaves. Some parents believe in due process, but is this clearly communicated to the child? What is the level of communication? I will ask the following questions: a) Do you read them their rights? (Example: "Son, things will probably go better for you if you tell me the truth."); b) Do you issue the charge? (Example: "The school called and reported that you missed 4th and 5th periods today."); c) Do you run the trial? (Example: "Tell me what happened."); d) Do you convict? (Example: "Skipping class is an egregious violation."); and e) Do you sentence? (Example: "You are grounded from all social events.") Or do you skip (a) through (d) and go straight to convict and sentence?

Also, do you explain or connect the reason for the discipline with the method used? For example: "Son, you know how important education is in this family, so you can take the time you would normally spend with your friends to grasp the importance of time in class."

Next is whether the method of discipline is specifically tailored for each child, or is a one-size-fits-all approach used? Some families have a hierarchy, and kids understand how it works. It could look something like this:

• Ordinance violation—disobeyed a household rule. Example: Watched TV w/o permission (core principle: obedience).

- Misdemeanors—disobeyed a parent's direct order. Example: Watched TV w/o permission instead of doing homework (core principle: obedience/ education).
- Felony 2—disobeyed a parent's direct order and placed themselves at some risk of harm. Example: Opened a cupboard and took a contraband ball outside to play after school without doing homework, then ran into the street to retrieve the ball without looking both ways (core principle: obedience/ safety violation; education).
- Felony 1 = a Felony 2, and lied about it. Example: Stood and denied the truth in the presence of the Neighbor who witnessed the incident as he gave his testimony (core principle: obedience/safety violation; education; honesty; respecting authority; respecting elders).
- Habitual violators—One or more of the above more than once.

How does the continuum work? And which one requires physical discipline?

Bias and the Need to Call Experts

One of the great minefields through which an attorney must maneuver is the psychological assessment that assists or persuades the court when making decisions on guilt/innocence, custody, placement, parenting time, or even the termination of parental rights, in terms of how to ensure equity. Each side calls an expert to advance its point of view. Psychological assessments appear to be objective because they use tests to support their findings and recommendations. However, African American parents usually don't fare well with mental health clinicians that don't approve of spanking, were never spanked, or were spanked and thought it was a barbaric, abusive disciplinary tactic. They bring their personal judgment into the analysis and conclusions. In order to challenge a psychological evaluation, it is necessary as an attorney to understand how cultural bias is not only built into the tests, but is also filtered through the opinions into the recommendations. And be prepared to not only contest the conclusions, but also the means and methods that were used in order to get them there. Questions must be asked about whether or not the test has been normed for African Americans, as well as how it should be properly applied in order to minimize racial and cultural bias. Consideration for calling your own expert should be ruled in or out early.

JACKSON CASE

On June 1, 2018, Monty Jackson whupped his stepson Kaleb with a belt on his bare bottom in the presence of a Child Protective Services worker. The next day, Trevor, a CPS investigator, came to the home and informed Monty that he was investigating a report of physical abuse and asked to see Kaleb's bare bottom. Monty refused, telling the investigator that the request was not appropriate and that he would take Kaleb to the doctor and have him examined instead. Monty did so on the same day, and provided a report to CPS. The doctor found no injuries. On June 7, 2018, the parents were hauled into court alleging that (1) Mr. Jackson used physical discipline upon Kaleb in the form of using a belt on Kaleb's bare buttocks at least twice; (2) Mr. Jackson had repeatedly used physical discipline upon Kaleb despite safety plans and service provider intervention; and (3) Mr. Jackson had stated that he would continue to use physical discipline. For good measure, an additional allegation was thrown in; (4) Mr. Jackson verbally threatened the service provider with violence. When they got into court, Monty was very angry about the assumption that he wasn't a fit parent. To the contrary, he said that he was a good parent and that he had a right to discipline his children as he saw fit. He wrote motions, and while they had no relevance to the case, he still wrote them. And he was very adamant about his case. At the preliminary hearing, the court ordered Mr. Jackson out of the home and continued the children in the home with their mother, Toni. Mr. Jackson was livid, and vehemently protested the court's action, to the point that he had to be escorted out of the building.

At the pretrial conference, Mr. Jackson demanded that his attorney do something or that he would represent himself. He continued his high-octane protestations, stating and restating that he had done nothing wrong and that he was a good parent. He also demanded a jury trial. He was doing most of this in a conference room with his attorney when security came in and told him to lower his voice. Mr. Jackson did not appreciate the admonition, and took the warning as a threat that required a negative response. The deputy took offense at his response and moved to arrest him on the spot. He instructed Mr. Jackson to place his hands behind his back, and when Mr. Jackson did not appear to comply, the deputy took the response as resisting and tried to force him to do so. Mr. Jackson repeatedly told him, "I can't, I am disabled." The deputy tazed him three times and took him to jail. As it turns out, his arms were bent at the elbows in a 45-degree angle. He was physically incapable of placing his hands behind his back. The PT was adjourned.

Mr. Jackson had an excellent court-appointed attorney who had prepared a jury demand and then filed it on Mr. Jackson's behalf. But Mr. Jackson was angry with everyone, including his attorney, and he shared his opinion with the court.

The next court date was the adjourned PT/Jury Trial Settlement Conference. Mr. Jackson indicated that he didn't want his lawyer and would appear pro se. This is when the court contacted me and asked if I would step in and replace his original appointed attorney. I agreed to do so. My first appearance was on

September 19, 2018, at the pretrial/jury trial Settlement Conference. At that point, I was filled in on all of the preliminary information. During our first meeting, I found Mr. Jackson intent on the fact that he knew his rights and neither wanted nor needed an attorney. But after our discussion, he agreed to allow me to help him.

Now he had a criminal case. While he was in jail, he had lost his job; he now had no kids in his care, and he was homeless. My first challenge was to cultivate a relationship with him and let him know that I respected him. I provided as much effort as I could in order to ensure that he had dignity in this process, and I made it as clear as possible that we could develop trust in one another. However, I knew that it would take time.

Client Interview

Our next meeting occurred at my office conference room. Monty arrived on time, but he was still skeptical. There was an extensive interview process. As we enjoyed a beverage together, he was unaware that we had actually begun to discuss the case. What appeared to be just friendly chatting was actually my working through my Best Practice Factors with him. He began to relax and get into the flow of our conversation. We talked about how he was raised and who his parents were. We discussed how they had disciplined him, and what they believed in. We then pivoted to how Monty's upbringing had formed his core principles. Finally, we talked about his and Toni's family, how it had initially formed, and who they were as parents. He was an intelligent young man with some college experience but who could not advance himself academically because he and Toni just couldn't afford it at that time. Later, we began to strategize about next steps. I suggested that I prepare an affidavit to provide to the court. I knew that they would have an expert witness, and I would request funds for one of our own. Their individual was a trauma expert who had never met a parent whose rights should not be terminated. (This is not hyperbolae. Over the past twenty years, I've cross-examined him at numerous Termination of Parental Rights trials, and have actually placed that testimony on the record.) The trial was set for December, and we had a great deal of work to do before that time. It was at that point Monty finally agreed he needed my help and that he was willing to allow me to represent him.

I explained that we would prepare an affidavit. Our goal was to challenge the racial assumptions that Monty was not a fit parent, as well as to establish the constitutional presumption that he is a fit parent who had also whupped his child. Finally, we had to legally challenge the abuse charges, and our affidavit would go a long way toward accomplishing these objectives. This affidavit would be provided to the court, the prosecution, and both expert witnesses.

We talked about Monty's family history and his parents. We talked about where he grew up, and we discussed how his parents had disciplined him. He told me that he had received whuppins from his mother. He always knew when he was in trouble, because he knew what made his mother mad. She hated lying, and he knew that lying was one of the worst things he could do. Did he consider his mother's treatment abusive? No, he did not consider it abusive. She really wanted him to be a good man who would have a good job when he grew up. His parents worked hard, but didn't have a lot of money. His socioeconomic status was actually pretty strong because he was willing to work hard as well, even though he was developmentally disabled. He was just in a bad situation at that time. He was very intelligent, but without a college degree. He enjoyed reading and researching what he needed to know, but lacked a formal education. He had core principles that were similar to those of his parents. In some ways, he wanted more for his kids because of how much things have changed. He did not want his kids in jail. He wanted them to graduate from college, no matter how hard it would be to accomplish that goal. And I used all of this information to establish his disciplinary practices.

Monty is the father of a little girl and the stepfather of two boys, and he and their mother resided together as a family since 2014. His son Kaleb had been having issues ever since he was very young. He was under a doctor's care, and the pediatrician had informed them two years before that Kaleb was too young to do diabetic testing but that they would keep an eye on him in order to see if the issue would correct itself. If not, they would do further testing to determine whether or not he was diabetic. Kaleb continued to regularly wet the bed at night. But his parents understood what the problems were, and that it was not his fault. They decided to establish the following protocols, because they wanted Kaleb to begin participating in self-care and to assume some responsibilities:

1. They would never have disciplined him physically or otherwise because he wet the bed or his clothes.
2. When he wet himself, he was expected to place his wet clothes and sheets in a plastic bag separate from the dirty clothes bag. The bag was hung on one of his bed posts.
3. He was expected to notify Monty or Toni so that he could take a shower with their help, and then he would put on clean clothes.

The parents had different means of discipline, and they tailored them to each of their children. They placed the children in a corner or sent them to their room. That was effective for Brian, because he hated being alone and didn't mind cleaning up. On the other hand, assigning chores was a more effective disciplinary method for Kaleb, because he hated to clean up. He had a great imagination and loved going to his room because he could go inside his head and do all kinds of fun things. He loved playing alone. All of the above methods were effective for Tisha, the youngest one, because she was social and she hated cleaning up. Family night exclusion was effective for all three children because that was their favorite activity. On family night, Monty, Toni, and the kids would watch a movie together with snacks and Kool-Aid or juice. They could be restricted to only water and no snacks or Kool-Aid or juice, or cancel family night altogether. Last on the continuum was corporal punishment.

Together, Toni and Monty demonstrated core family principles. They believed in *honesty, trust, commitment, effective communication, God, education, not accepting failure, respect*, and *love*. On the day in question, the caseworker was present in the home to close an informal case that had been opened regarding Toni. During the visit, Toni said she thought that Kaleb had peed on himself. Although he had dry clothes on, Toni could still smell it. When Monty asked Kaleb if he had peed on himself, Kaleb lied and denied that he had done so, which was a big violation of core principles. Monty and Toni emphasized that in their household, they believed that God and honesty were the bedrocks upon which all other core principles were built.

Under further investigation, they discovered that Kaleb had put on clean clothes over his wet clothes. He had violated the protocol and then lied about it. The parents had taught Kaleb how to follow the protocol, and he understood what he was supposed to do. He knew that it was wrong to lie, especially to his parents or other adults. Monty stood and very calmly escorted Kaleb to his room, and with Kaleb's belt, Monty gave him two licks on his buttocks. But then the caseworker informed Monty that he had violated the safety plan by using physical discipline. Monty informed her that he had a right to whup his kids and that he would continue to whup them when they needed it. The caseworker subsequently left the home and filed a complaint. On the following day, the CPS investigator arrived and asked to see Kaleb's bare buttocks. Monty would not allow this, but he said that he would take Kaleb to see his pediatrician that same day.

Our county court requires prior approval for expert witness fees, and it took about a month to get the order. Winter had set in early that year, and my client had been ordered out of the home and was temporarily homeless. He was forced to couch-surf in order to continue to help providing for the family, because they could not afford two homes. It was accordingly quite difficult to get in touch with him. After preparing the affidavit, I picked him up at a McDonald's location downtown and transported him to my office in order to review and notarize the document. The following affidavit was filed with the court and appropriately disseminated to both expert witnesses and the prosecutor.

CASE STUDY

STATE OF XXXX

IN THE MATTER OF: Brian J; Kaleb L; and Tisha J

* * * * * * * *

Affidavit

STATE OF XXXX)
)ss.
XXX COUNTY)

    NOW COMES the Affiant, Monty J, and states:

1. I am the father of Tisha J, d.o.b. 4-25-2016.
2. I am the stepfather of Brian J (10/02/2011); and Kaleb L (11/20/2013).
3. I and their mother, Toni L, have resided together with the children as a family since approximately February, 2014.
4. Kaleb has been examined since he was three years old, as he has been symptomatic of diabetes and a genetic disorder due to excessive thirst and bed wetting.
5. As Kaleb wets the bed every night, at age 4, his mother and I established a protocol so that he could participate in self-care around his bed and clothes wetting: when he wets himself and/or his bed, he was to: a) place his wet clothes/sheets in a plastic bag separate from the dirty clothes bag; b) notify one of us before; c) taking a shower; and d) putting on clean clothes.
6. We do not discipline Kaleb or any of the children for bedwetting or wetting themselves.
7. As a means of discipline, we use various methods and tailor our methods to be most effective for each child:
   a. Sitting in a corner or being sent to his room, which is most effective for Brian, because he hates being alone and doesn't mind cleaning up.
   b. Assigning chores, which is a more effective disciplinary tactic for Kaleb, because he hates to clean up; he has a great imagination, and he loves going to his room to play alone.

   c. All of the above are effective for Tisha.

   d. No family night or being excluded from family night activities, such as watching a movie together.

   e. Allowing water only (not allowing juice, Kool-Aid or snacks).

   f. Corporal punishment as a last resort.

8. Toni and I have a set of core principles that we try to live by and teach to the children:

   a. Honesty

   b. Trust

   c. Commitment

   d. Effective communication

   e. God

   f. Education

   g. Not accepting failure

   h. Respect

   i. Love

9. On June 1, 2018, the CPS worker was at our house to close a case on Toni.

10. During the visit, Toni said that she thought that Kaleb had peed on himself.

11. Although he had dry clothes on, Toni said she could smell it.

12. When I asked him if he had peed on himself, Kaleb denied that he had done so.

13. Under further investigation, I discovered that Kaleb had put on clean clothes over wet underwear, and was lying about it.

14. I spanked him twice on his behind using his belt.

15. I then put him in the shower.

16. On the following day, Trevor M arrived at the house and asked that I pull Kaleb's pants down so that he could see his butt.

17. I did not think that was appropriate, and told him that I would take Kaleb to the doctor that day for an examination.

18. I took Kaleb to the doctor that same day, and there was no indication of injuries.

FURTHER AFFIANT SAITH NOT.

Trial Prep

One major use of the affidavit was to provide my expert with some context for our side of the case. She had no need to interview my client once this information had been provided. She conducted her own research, and we met for witness preparation. After our meeting, our expert prepared her report, and after reviewing the court files and our affidavit, she concluded that:

> The court considers CPS investigations when making decisions on child abuse cases. CPS failed to provide a culturally responsive, comprehensive, evidenced-based report to substantiate their findings that Mr. Jackson's disciplinary practices are problematic and/or abusive.

The goal of the affidavit was to (1) challenge the assumption that Monty was not a fit father; (2) rebut the presumption that he was unfit; and (3) challenge the charge that he had crossed the line from discipline to abuse. We believed that this affidavit successfully satisfied the first two objectives. But even using Best Interest Factors and Disciplinary Best Practice Factors, deciding whether or not a parent is not fit is subjective. I was confident that we would be able to show that Monty was a fit father, because fit parents have established plans and processes when addressing discipline in their households. But we still had to go to trial and legally challenge the charges of abuse. The affidavit was also helpful in rebutting some of the poor reputation that Monty had earned around the court house. We were able to offer evidence that Monty was not just a wild, crazy, and unreasonable guy who had to be tazed into submission. In spite of his courthouse antics, he was a thoughtful parent who put time and effort into the work of parenting and disciplining his children.

The next objective was to lay the groundwork in order to legally challenge the charges, and we were successful in that area as well. The prosecutor's expert witness reviewed both our affidavit and our expert's report, and on the day of trial, he informed the prosecutor that he wouldn't be of any assistance and that there was no point in him testifying. He didn't disagree with anything that our expert said, especially in lieu of what the parent had stated in the affidavit. He further stated that "it doesn't sound like this guy is out of control. Plus, there was never any bruising."

Trial Day

At trial, our expert provided unchallenged testimony. We cross-examined the caseworker who had been present on the day of the spanking with regard to why she didn't ask the question "why?" in order to gain context for the disciplinary action. She testified that the physical discipline violated the Service Agreement and Safety Plan, and that Mr. Jackson said that he would continue to do so. She had no choice but to file a complaint (per policy).

The CPS investigator who questioned the parents testified that he was provided with medical documentation that there was no evidence of abuse. He too was probed with regard to why, during his investigation, he had failed to inquire into the circumstances of the physical discipline. He had no plausible explanation, yet he continued to attempt to paint Monty as violent and threatening toward him.

Monty testified to the information presented on the affidavit, and he was able to expand upon how he parented, reiterating that the core principles of the family were behind the disciplinary rationale. Toni testified about the protocol for Kaleb's self-care as well. The court found in our favor and dismissed the case regarding my client.

Chapter 7

Recommendations and Implications for Future Research, Training, and Practice

This book has established that African American parents use a variety of disciplinary methods in order to address child misbehavior, and that these strategies are often predicated by the age of the child and the context of the disciplinary episode. This work underscores the importance of obtaining the parenting viewpoints of African American fathers as well as mothers in conceptualizing child discipline in African American homes. This information provided a culturally responsive framework(s) for clinicians, child welfare workers, and legal professionals to better articulate and affirm what is *normal*, *necessary*, and *functional* when addressing the phenomenon of child discipline in African American families. The perspectives from a trial lawyer in this book demonstrated how the ideas and arguments made in this book are played out in a real-world context. The African American father illustrated in Chapter 6 was dehumanized in the legal system and was prevented for a period of time from living with and seeing his children. Had the human service professional(s) involved utilized a contextualized humanistic approach to their service delivery, they would have perceived Mr. William's parenting as a creative approach to addressing the developmental needs of his son and that the family would not have experienced a traumatic separation.

Additionally, clear from this body of work is that the presumption that African American parents are "preoccupied with hitting their children" or "child-abusing disciplinarians" is wrong, and is not at all supported by scientific evidence. Specifically, this discussion provided a detailed and comprehensive portrait of how African American mothers and African American fathers respond both individually and as a team to address repeated misbehavior in their children. Disciplinary patterns in African American homes were found to be hierarchal in nature, meaning that verbal discussions are typically the first response, and then escalate to more coercive strategies as needed (e.g., the withdrawal of privileges, giving the child a warning look) in order to address repeated misconduct. When and if physical discipline is used (with an open hand or the use of a belt), it is rarely handled as a stand-alone strategy.

The voices of African American parents shared in this book offer an important corrective to the dehumanized view of African American mothers and fathers that is so often found in child welfare and social science periodicals (Johnson, 2006). Respectively, parenting programs and methods used by social workers and mental health professionals in order to assess child discipline should be reflective of the ways in which African American parents actually discipline their children.

In order to encourage more African American participation in agency programming, father-only support and/or counseling groups could be offered to better address the parenting concerns of African American fathers. It is also important to recognize that this book identified a collaborative process in how African American mothers and fathers address repeated misbehavior in their children. Thus, various helping professionals (e.g., social workers, clinicians, guardian ad litem) may need to interview African American mothers and fathers together in order to clearly delineate child-rearing competencies in African American families.

It is also important to note that the child discipline information presented in this book can also inform programming for families involved in the juvenile court system. Mothers and fathers can be overwhelmed by life demands, socioeconomic realities, and unresolved emotional issues that could impact the behavior of their children. For parents who have children in the juvenile justice system, the task of addressing these life demands is further complicated by their interaction with external systems (agencies, schools, legal system). Few parent education programs address the needs of families with adolescent children and even less focus on mothers and fathers who are currently experiencing behavioral problems with their teenagers.

For three years I worked with Ms. Juanita Newsome, an African American family interventionist/probation officer to develop and implement a psychoeducational counseling group for parents who had a child involved with juvenile court. Most of these families struggled financially and had fallen between the cracks of the social service system. This program was based on Ms. Newsome's thirty-plus years of experience working with complex and high-need families of young offenders and my research presented in this book. This group intervention assumes that all parents who participate are competent and want what is best for their children. Parents engage in deep introspective counseling while examining what is normal, necessary, and functional in addressing adolescent problematic behavior. This psychoeducational group approach provides a path for the clinician to assess the cause and maintenance of disciplinary problems within the parenting system for each group member (Adkison-Johnson, 2015;

Adkison-Johnson & Payne, 2019). The family interventionist found that families of young offenders grappled with ordinary teenage behavioral problems, but were also overwhelmed with economic issues and navigating external systems that often perceived parents of color as the cause of their children's dysfunction (Newsome personal communication, 2016). Many parents were also challenged by their own negative childhood disciplinary experiences (inconsistent rules, blurred boundaries, victims of child abuse) which compromised their ability to establish firm guidelines with their children.

PARENT COUNSELING GROUP SESSIONS

We found that a ten-week session format is most appealing to parents which also accommodates more in-depth introspection for larger groups (eight to ten members). Each session met once a week for ninety minutes. Each group was closed to new members before the beginning of the first counseling session to encourage group cohesion. I facilitated each counseling session while Ms. Newsome kept in communication with the families between sessions to reaffirm the concepts and strategies discussed in the group counseling sessions. She also served as a buffer between the parents and external systems (ex. family and criminal courts, Department of Human Services) to provide space for parents to grow and be vulnerable while reflecting on their child-rearing goals and practices.

Sessions One and Two

The initial sessions of the parent counseling group focused on parents distinguishing adolescent behaviors they considered as problematic. The goal of the initial phase is to establish an atmosphere where group members can speak freely about inappropriate behaviors in adolescent children and where their own children have "crossed the line" with them. This is an important step in understanding the child-rearing priorities and desires of each parent. It likewise recognizes the parents' capabilities in raising their children.

Sessions Three and Four

These sessions concentrated on disciplinary methods used by parents to shape their children's behavior. Specifically, parents were encouraged to reflect on their socialization practices at each stage of their child's development (preschool, elementary, adolescent) pinpointing how children were taught to interact within the family and the larger society. The following questions generated insightful dialogue within the group:

How would you like your child to function as an adult?

What types of disciplinary methods, experiences and resources are you using to prepare your child for adulthood?

How do you distinguish between child discipline and child abuse?

Sessions Four and Five

During the middle phase of the group intervention, parents reflect on their own childhood experiences in relation to child discipline. As mentioned earlier in this book, parents who were troubled by the ways in which they were disciplined as children often refused to use any form of firm discipline with their own children. We found that when a parent experienced child abuse during their developmental years, they often struggled with setting firm limits or boundaries with their adolescent children. Emphasis is placed on the meaning each parent made of their childhood experiences that may have caused emotional pain. The goal of this session was for the parent to distinguish between the origin of their emotional struggles and their reaction to their child's misbehavior. The following questions were helpful in engaging parents in deep introspective reflection:

How were you disciplined as a child?

Were there any disciplinary experiences that were not effective or painful?

Were there any disciplinary experiences that impacted your life in a positive way?

What disciplinary methods from childhood are you currently using with your own children?

It is important that the clinician be trained to address emotional pain. Moreover, the group facilitator should be able to recognize a range of responses to trauma so that appropriate referrals to culturally responsive individual counseling can be provided to group members.

Sessions Six and Seven

These sessions provide an opportunity for the parents to reflect on how they might have "let their child down" or disappointed them in the past. These sessions also begin the process of parents evaluating their current relationship with their adolescent that is involved in the court system. The purpose of this phase of counseling is to provide an opportunity for each parent to reflect on their feelings, guilt, and intentions that might have adversely impacted their children. This helps parents to establish insight into their own intentions and that feelings of regret from parenting missteps can be appropriately addressed with their children. According to Hardy & Laszloffy (2003) parents who are intentional about reflecting on their own childhood experiences as well as their lives as parents have an easier time restoring relationships with their adolescent children.

Sessions Eight, Nine, and Ten

The last phase of the group focuses on assisting mothers and fathers with establishing boundaries in accordance with their parenting goals and house rules. Parents are cautioned that this will take time. However, when parents reach this phase of counseling they are less anxious and more flexible about the resistance they may face from their children.

Overall, the parents' heart, intentions, and agency are valued and strengthened during their time in group. The group highlights the parents' capacity to appropriately intervene in the lives of their teenagers. Mothers and fathers who have participated in the parent group experience feel heard and empowered. Information drawn from the parent participation in group can serve as a guide for court officials to make suitable and culturally appropriate guidelines and recommendations for youth and families who live in an increasingly diverse society.

Helping professionals from various disciplines are ethically bound to embrace a counseling approach that supports the worth, dignity, potential, and uniqueness of clients within their social and cultural contexts (e.g., American Counseling Association Code of Ethics, 2005). As such, it is essential for clinicians and child welfare workers, when interpreting the disciplinary practices of parents, to understand not only the disciplinary strategy used by the parent, but also the context of the disciplinary episode, the intent and/or behavioral expectation of the parent, and the development of the child as a member of his or her cultural group (Thomas & Dettlaff, 2011).

There are many unanswered questions regarding the disciplinary strategies used by African American parents. For instance, what is the long-term effect of using a continuum approach to child discipline? Specifically, does this particular approach produce the adult behaviors desired by the parent? Future investigations could examine the impact of parental expectations on the disciplinary strategies used by African American parents. This information would be useful in studying the effects of African American parenting on the lives of African American children. Additionally, a more controversial question such as the impact of using physical discipline as a last resort parenting method may also need to be closely examined. As stated in the book introduction, several professional organizations have issued anti-spanking mandates with virtually no supporting data that establishes a cause-and-effect relationship within African American families. Future investigations that provide a detailed analysis on using physical discipline as the last resort would provide more insight into this contentious issue.

The results from this book could also expand curricular and clinical training with African American mothers and fathers in master's and doctoral counseling, psychology, and social work programs. Being committed to social justice and understanding the importance of multicultural awareness as a clinician or social worker is necessary but also woefully insufficient in working with African American clients. It is crucial that graduate training programs require students to obtain documented and supervised clinical experiences with African American men and women (mothers and fathers) before graduating. Future studies may attempt to examine the perspectives of faculty and supervisors in order to assess their level of knowledge and skill in the area of parenting in general, as well as child rearing in racial minority families in particular. This information would be valuable in designing appropriate continuing education training for faculty and clinical supervisors in order to acquire or update their skills in providing responsive supervision and curricular experiences to clinicians and social workers in training.

Another emerging issue will be the counseling, psychology, and social work professions' response to African American parents impacted by COVID-19. I am writing the conclusion of this book in the midst of the COVID-19 crisis in our country. Right now, the majority of children and families across the United States are required "to shelter in place" for protection from this devastating virus outbreak. Schools have moved to remote learning, knowing full well that not all children have access to computers or even the internet. Many parents of color, who are often at risk for being "last hired and first fired," have been placed on furlough, laid off, or fired because of lack of childcare, struggling with the virus themselves, or dealing with a family member who has fallen ill or even died from the complications of COVID-19.

Parents are currently having to deal with a multitude of crisis both at home and in their community with very little resources or support, and are doing the best they can with whatever they have. I wonder how this crisis is impacting African American mothers and fathers. Will they reach out for help, knowing that helping professionals struggle to see them as competent parents? Do they risk admitting failures and mistakes in disciplining their children (if they occurred) due to fears that child welfare will remove their children based on the flawed assumption that "parenting while Black means that children are at risk of being harmed?"

However, a grave issue that is at the forefront for many African American parents is the vicious murders of African American men, women, and children by law enforcement and civilians whose actions are justified and protected by state officials. White supremacy is not a new phenomenon for African Americans who suffered through several centuries of chattel slavery in the United States.

Earlier in this book it was emphasized that racial socialization is one of the cornerstones of child rearing for African American parents. To protect children from the effects of White supremacy, African American parents provide racially specific strategies to prepare their children to thrive in a society that is racist toward African Americans (Stevenson et al., 2001; Mc Neil et al., 2014). However, it is clear that although most children within African American families have received some messages about being African American in a racist society, racial socialization alone may not be enough to save their lives.

There is an urgency right now to help African American children understand why they are being victimized and murdered, why their own parents may be victimized and murdered as well. I was excited to find the clinical intervention work of Anderson et al. (2019). Specifically, their Engraving, Managing, and Bonding through Race (EMBRace) counseling model empowers African American youth and families to confront racism together. It also provides African American youth and families with tools and skills to resolve racial trauma and reduce racial stress in an effort to promote healthy coping for racial encounters. EMBRace is designed for parents and adolescents to receive individual counseling. Parents and adolescents also work in dyads and sessions are implemented by trained clinicians. The work of Anderson et al. has been supported by funding by the National Institutes of Health.

Helping professions must anticipate and clearly articulate to the public that they are willing and able to assist African American families in times of crisis, and a starting point for all of this is actually seeing African American mothers and fathers as capable of being competent parents.

REFERENCES

Adkison-Johnson, C., & Payne, D. (2019). *Criminality vs. Intentionality: An Examination of the Disciplinary Practices of African American Parents.* Association of Family and Conciliation Courts 56th Annual Conference. Toronto, Canada.

Anderson, R. E., McKenny M. C., & Stevenson, H. C. (2019). EMBRace: Developing a racial socialization intervention to reduce racial stress and enhance racial coping among Black parents and adolescents. *Family Process, 58*(1), 53–64.

Hardy, K. V., & Laszloffy, T. A. (2005). *Teens Who Hurt: Clinical Interventions to Break the Cycle of Adolescent Violence.* New York: The Guilford Press.

Johnson, P. D. (2006). Counseling Black men: A contextualized humanistic approach. *Counseling and Values, 50,* 187–196. doi:10.1002/j.2161-007X.2006.tb00055.x

Thomas, K. A., & Dettlaff, A. J. (2011). African American families and the role of physical witnessing in the past in the present. *Journal of Human Behavior in the Social Environment, 21,* 963–977.

Index

AACD. *See* African American Child Discipline (AACD) Survey

ABA. *See* American Bar Association (ABA)

abuse. *See* child abuse

ACA. *See* American Counseling Association (ACA)

accountability, 57; punishment *versus*, 57

active parenting, of fathers, 49

adjusting child behavior, 53–55, *54*

Adkison-Johnson, C., 8

Adler, Alfred, 20–21

adolescent children, 37, 41–42; externalizing behaviors of, 36; fathers of, 48, 51; rebellious behaviors of, 40; respect for authority of, 58

AFCC. *See* Association of Family and Conciliation Courts (AFCC)

African American Child Discipline (AACD) Survey, 9, 51

aggressive behavior, 22

Akbar, Naim, 6, 52

Akinware, M., 18

Alford, K. A., 26, 27, 41

American Bar Association (ABA), 3

American Counseling Association (ACA), 76; Code of Ethics, 115

American Psychological Association (APA), 2, 35

American Psychologist (journal), 2

Anderson, John E., 34

Anderson, R. E., 117

anger, toward CPS, 83

Anglo-centric policies, 3

anti-spanking, 3, 73, 115

APA. *See* American Psychological Association (APA)

Arnold, Mary Smith, 6

Association of Family and Conciliation Courts (AFCC), 3

authoritarian control, 22

authoritative control, 22

authority: fathers and, 52–53; respect for, 58

Bandura, Albert, 21, 22

Barnes, A. S., 25, 26

Baumrind, D., 22

behavior: adjusting, 53–55, *54*; aggressive, 22; externalizing, 35–36; rebellious, 40

Best Interest Factors (BIF), 91–93

bias: court cases and, 101; cultural, 3, 9, 101; explicit, 90–91

BIF. *See* Best Interest Factors (BIF)

Billingsley, Andrew, 6, 17, 24

democratic approach, to discipline, 20
Denby, R. W., 26, 27, 41
Department of Health and Human
  Services (DHHS), 49, 96, 97
desertion, by fathers, 24
DeVet, K. A., 41
DHHS. *See* Department of Health and
  Human Services (DHHS)
dignity, 98–99
disagreements, in co-parenting, 66–67
Disciplinary Best Practice Factors
  (DBPF), 93–96
discipline. *See specific topics*
discussions with children, 1–2, 26, 67;
  by fathers, 51, 64; intentional, 40–42
disrespect, 25
distrust, in CPS, 83
Doctorate of Philosophy in Counseling
  and Development, 6
domestic court cases, 91
Doyle, O., 55, 63
Dreikurs, Rudolf, 20–21
DuBois, W. E. B., 19, 24

elementary-age children, 37, 51
EMBRace. *See* Engraving, Managing,
  and Bonding through Race
  (EMBRace)
emotional pain, 114
emotional support, by fathers, 48–49
empowerment phase, of counseling, 82,
  84
Engraving, Managing, and Bonding
  through Race (EMBRace), 117
errands, 18
experts, 101
explicit bias, 90–91
expunction, 97
extended family, 19
extensive interview questions, 99–101
externalizing behaviors, 35–36
extreme physical abuse, 90

families: blended, 69; counseling, 20;
  extended, 19; history, 99; middle-

class, 48; slave, 18; working-class,
  48
Family Team Meeting, 97
fathers, 47–48; active parenting of, 49;
  adjusting child behavior and, 53–55,
  54; of adolescent children, 48, 51;
  authority and, 52–53; desertion by,
  24; discipline by, 50–52; discussions
  by, 51, 64; emotional support by,
  48–49; narrative in detail for, 55–59;
  non-custodial, 48–50; non-resident,
  63–64; social fathering, 50, 53
felonies, 101
female slaves, 18
Fontes, L. A., 78
Forehand, R., 64
Franklin, J. H., 19
Frazier, E. F., 24
future research, training, and practice,
  111–13; parent counseling group
  sessions, 113–17

Garner, P., 35, 37
George, C., 50
God, 19
Golden Towers, 25
good manners, 25
good person (Omoluwabi), 17
Gordon, Thomas, 21
Greene, K., 35, 37

Halgunseth, L. C., 36, 37
Hamer, J. F., 48, 49
Hardy, Kenneth V., 6, 40, 58, 67, 114
hierarchal, disciplinary patterns as, 1,
  111
Hill, 78
Hill, R., 25
Hill-Collins, Patricia, 6, 34
historical perspectives, on child
  development post-slavery, 20–23
history, family, 99
Horn, I. B., 37
Houser, R. F., 18
humanistic approach, 7

About the Author

Carla Adkison-Johnson is a tenured professor and interim chairperson for the Department of Counselor Education and Counseling Psychology at Western Michigan University (WMU). She has a Ph.D. in Counseling and Human Development from Kent State University. She has published extensively in the areas of child discipline, culturally competent mental health counseling, and African American child-rearing practices. Dr. Adkison-Johnson is Editor-in-Chief of the *Journal of Multicultural Counseling and Development*. Her research has garnered attention in the legal, child welfare, and counselor education literature. She has served as a child discipline expert witness in civil and criminal courts. In 2017, she received the WMU College of Education and Human Development Distinguished Scholar Award. Dr. Adkison-Johnson is also the recipient of the Kent State University Outstanding Alumnus Award. She is a past member of the Board of Directors for the Council for Counseling and Educational Related Programs (CACREP), the national and international accrediting body for the counseling profession. In this capacity, she served as chair of CACREP's Training Committee. She has provided mental health counseling to the African American community for over thirty years.

Ingram Content Group UK Ltd.
Milton Keynes UK
UKHW040756250423
420747UK00004B/223

9 781793 620958